Old Grasmere and Rydal
Neil Honeyman

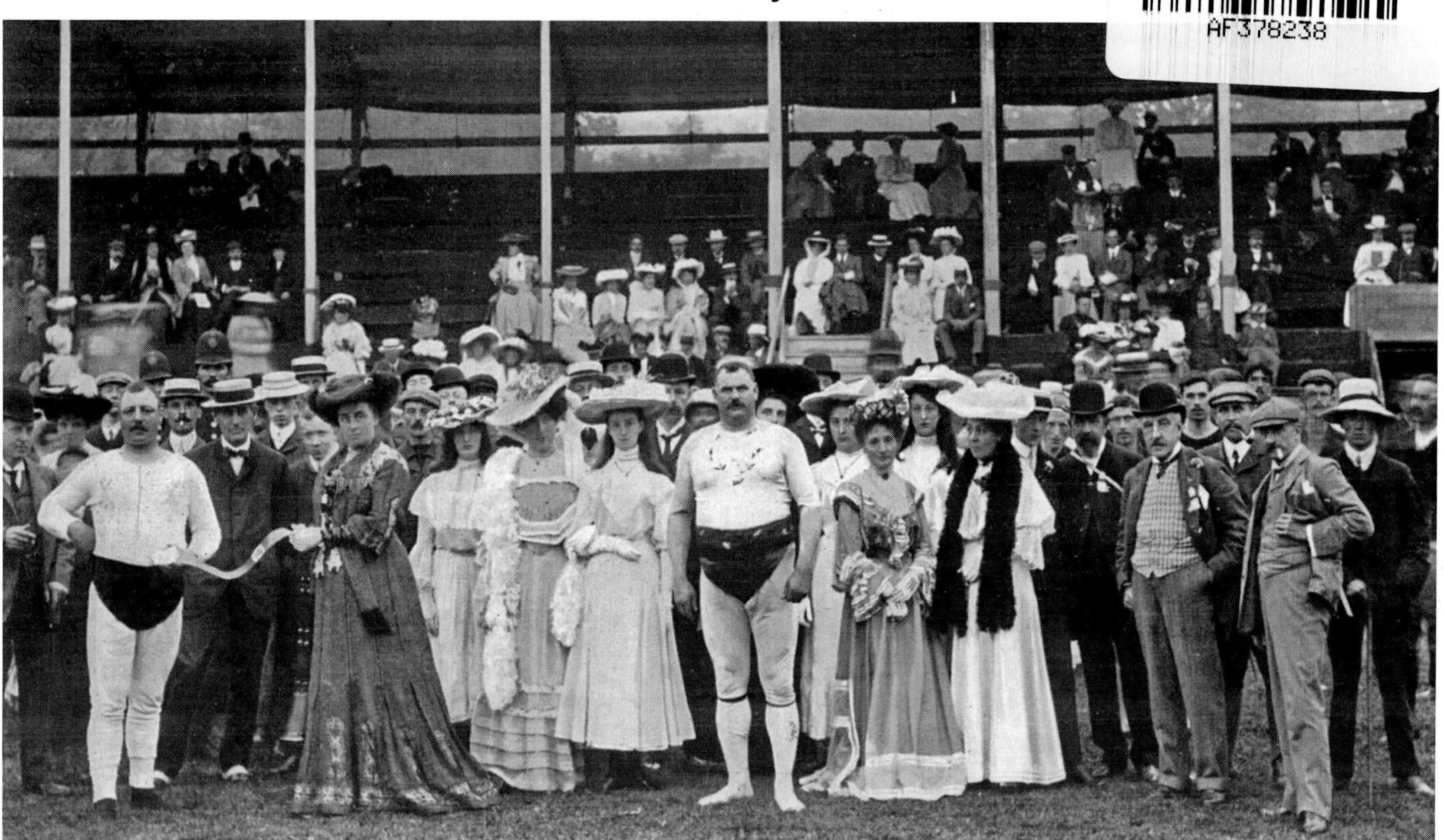

The official party make the presentations to the wrestling champions at the Grasmere Sports in 1903. The man on the left on the front row is Dick Howe, the famous and humorous Bellman, who was the Grasmere town crier for 40 years and was also the announcer at the Grasmere Sports for 27 years, in the days before loudspeakers! His last appearance there came in 1921, when he was 79.

INTRODUCTION

Every year, thousands of tourists flock to the neighbouring villages of Grasmere and Rydal to enjoy this popular Lakeland "hotspot", to ramble amongst the nearby tarns and fells, to admire the picturesque cottages or to browse in the many gift shops, or simply to enjoy a drink in one of the village cafes or pubs. Many visitors are drawn to the area because of its association with the poet William Wordsworth.

This book is intended neither as a history of Grasmere and Rydal and the surrounding area, nor as a biography of William Wordsworth: there is no shortage of guidebooks out there, and the internet is awash with information. Rather, it is hoped that this short book will give the reader a glimpse of life in Grasmere, Rydal and the nearby fells at the turn of the last century. Most of the illustrations are taken from old picture postcards, first used in Britain from 1893, and popular until the Second World War.

ACKNOWLEDGEMENTS

For many years, I have collected, and dealt in, old picture postcards, specialising in views of Old Lakeland. I have used some of my own cards for this book, but I am greatly indebted to Alan Stephenson, a native of Ambleside, who has kindly lent me his postcard collection and other material the better to illustrate *Old Grasmere and Rydal*. I would also like to thank my brother, Ian, who shares my love of the Lake District, and who has conscientiously proofread the books I have written and has suggested corrections. My wife, Sylvia, has once again supported me patiently in my research for this book. The factual errors – and I am sure there will be some – are mine alone, and I should be happy to stand corrected.

Also by Neil Honeyman and available from Stenlake Publishing.

Coast to Coast in the 1920s
Old Mardale
Old Hawkshead and Sawrey

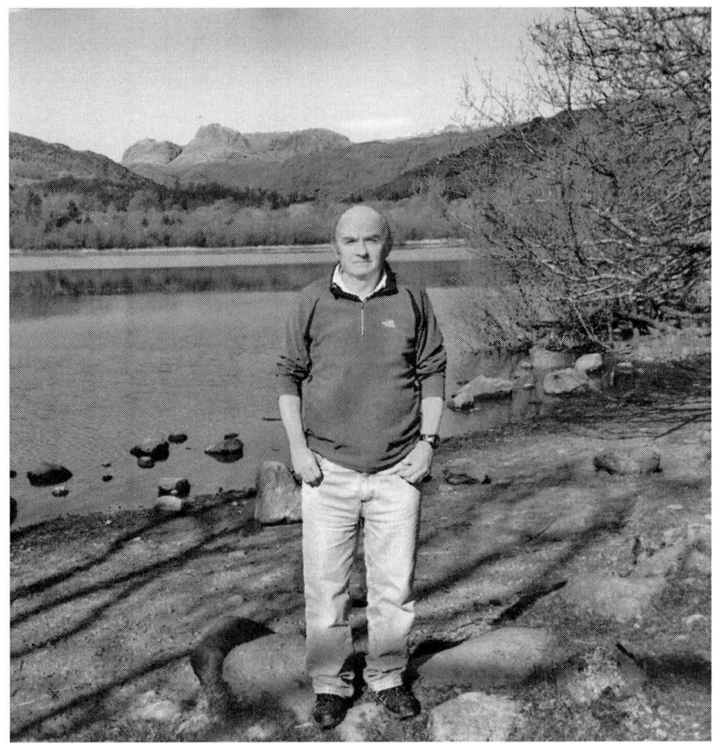

Alan Stephenson

© Neil Honeyman, 2017
First published in the United Kingdom, 2017,
by Stenlake Publishing Ltd.
www.stenlake.co.uk
ISBN 9781840337709

The publishers regret that they cannot supply
copies of any pictures featured in this book.

Printed by Blissetts, Roslin Road, Acton, W3 8DH

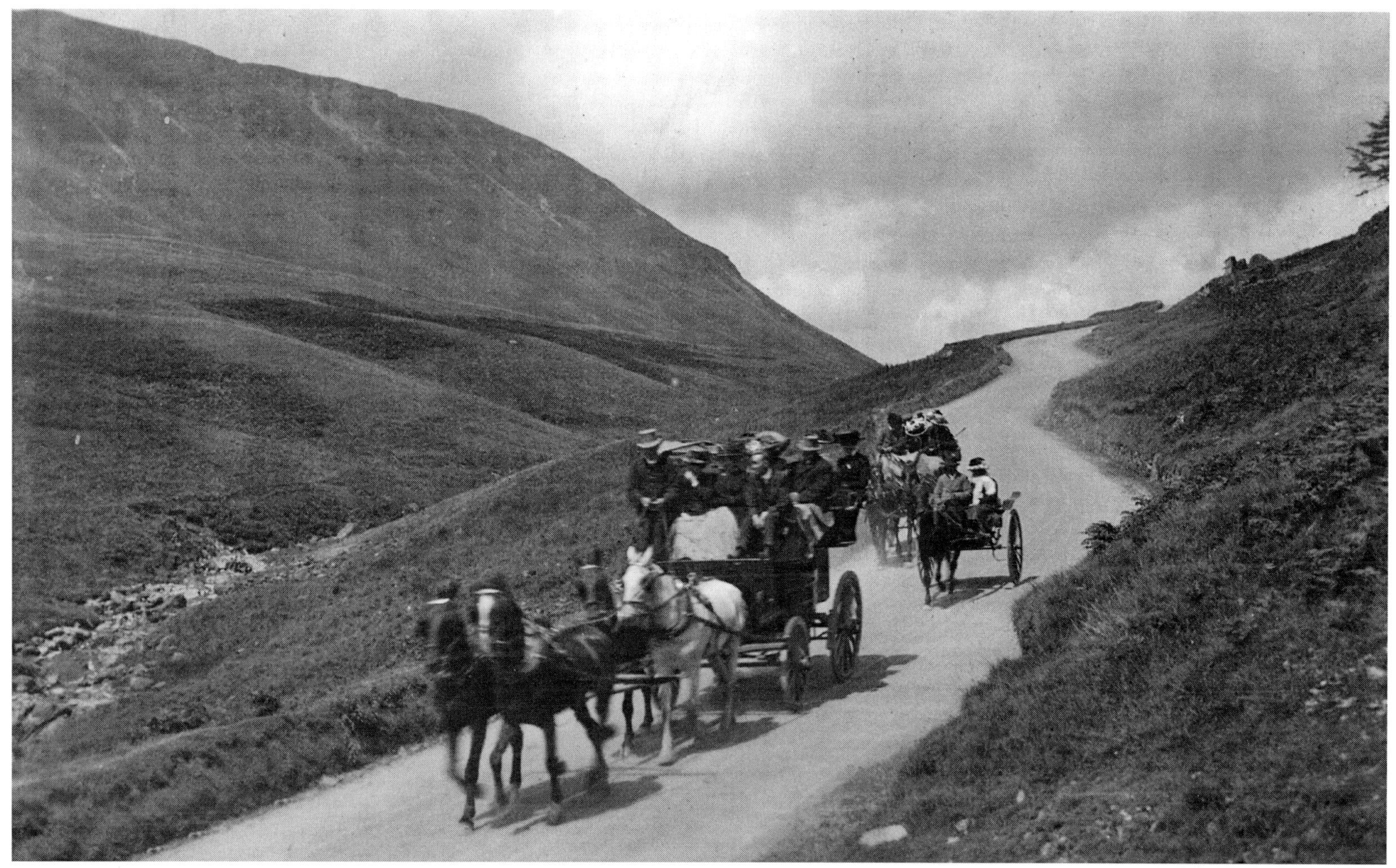

This early Pettitt of Keswick postcard shows groups of tourists making the steep descent from Dunmail Raise to Grasmere at the turn of the last century. The heavier coaches often left their mark on the unmetalled road, as chains and skids were used to immobilise a rear wheel and so to slow down the coach on steep hills, thereby preventing accidents. The pass was not always a peaceful route through the Lake District, for in the tenth century a battle was fought near here between the Cumbrians and the Northumbrians. The last Cumbrian king, Dunmail, died in the battle, his kingdom becoming part of Scotland, but his name will always be remembered by those who use the pass.

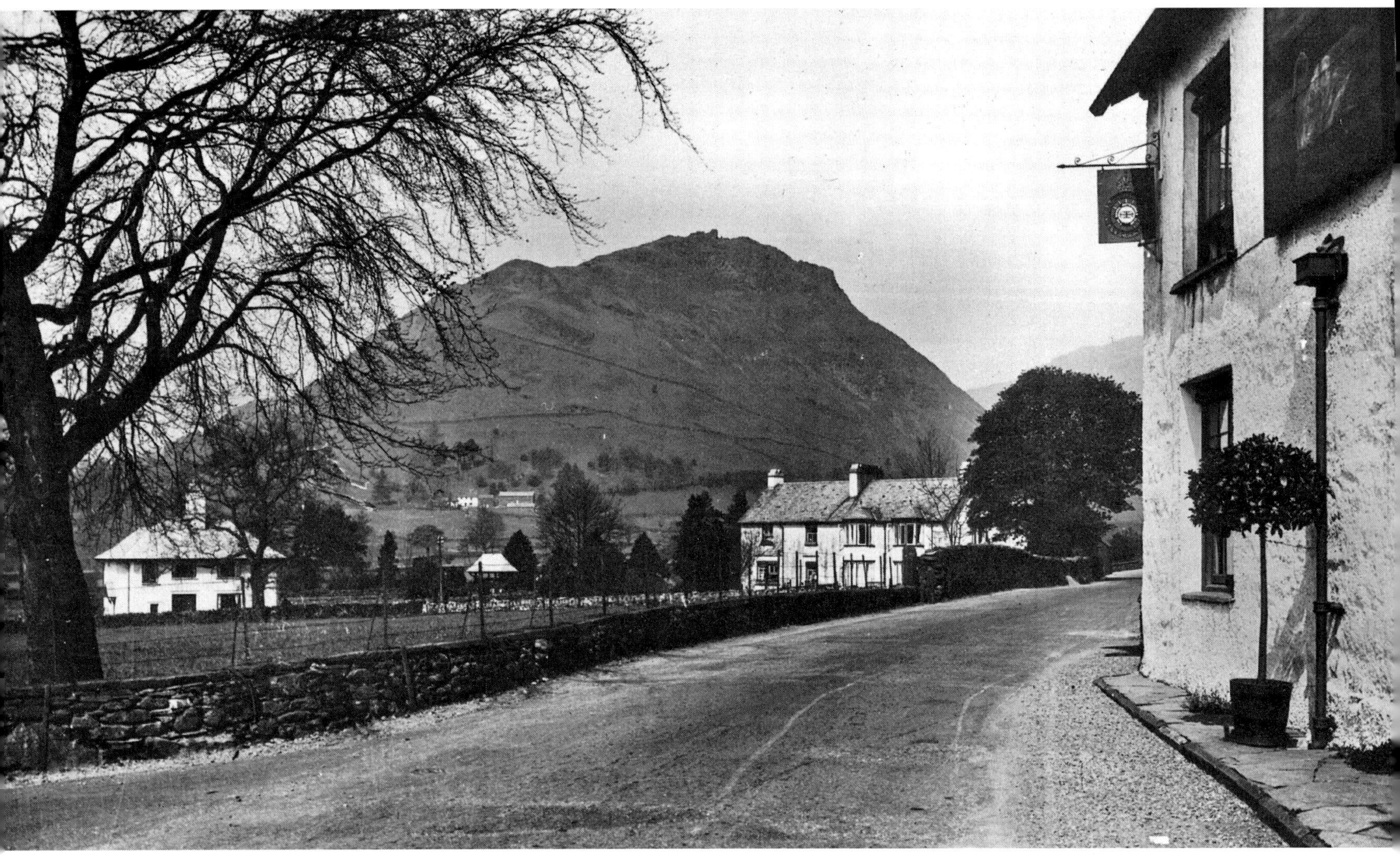

Travellers from Keswick would soon glimpse Helm Crag, which dominates the village of Grasmere. Fellwalkers know that the shapeless tumble of boulders and rocks on the summit, viewed from the road, take on the shape of a lion and a lamb or, from some angles, a lady playing an organ! The card carries a message: "Climbed this the first Sunday – sat on top of lamb."

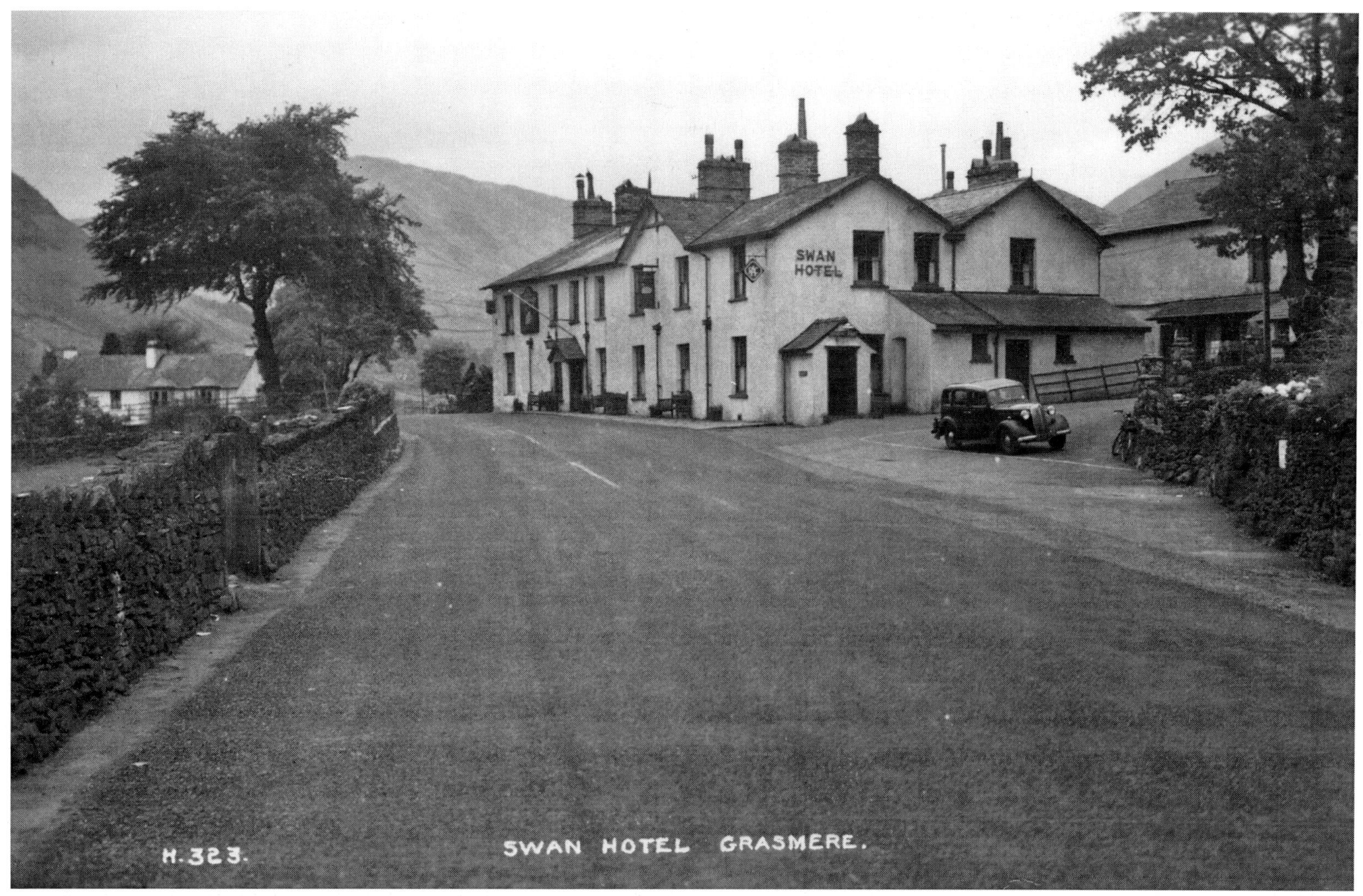

The Swan Hotel is an old and renowned coaching inn situated on the outskirts of Grasmere village, on the road from Keswick to Ambleside. The inn dates from about 1650, and it was mentioned in Wordsworth's poem *The Waggoner*. The sender of this card wrote: "Came to stay here for a week, last Friday, a very good hotel surrounded by beautiful scenery."

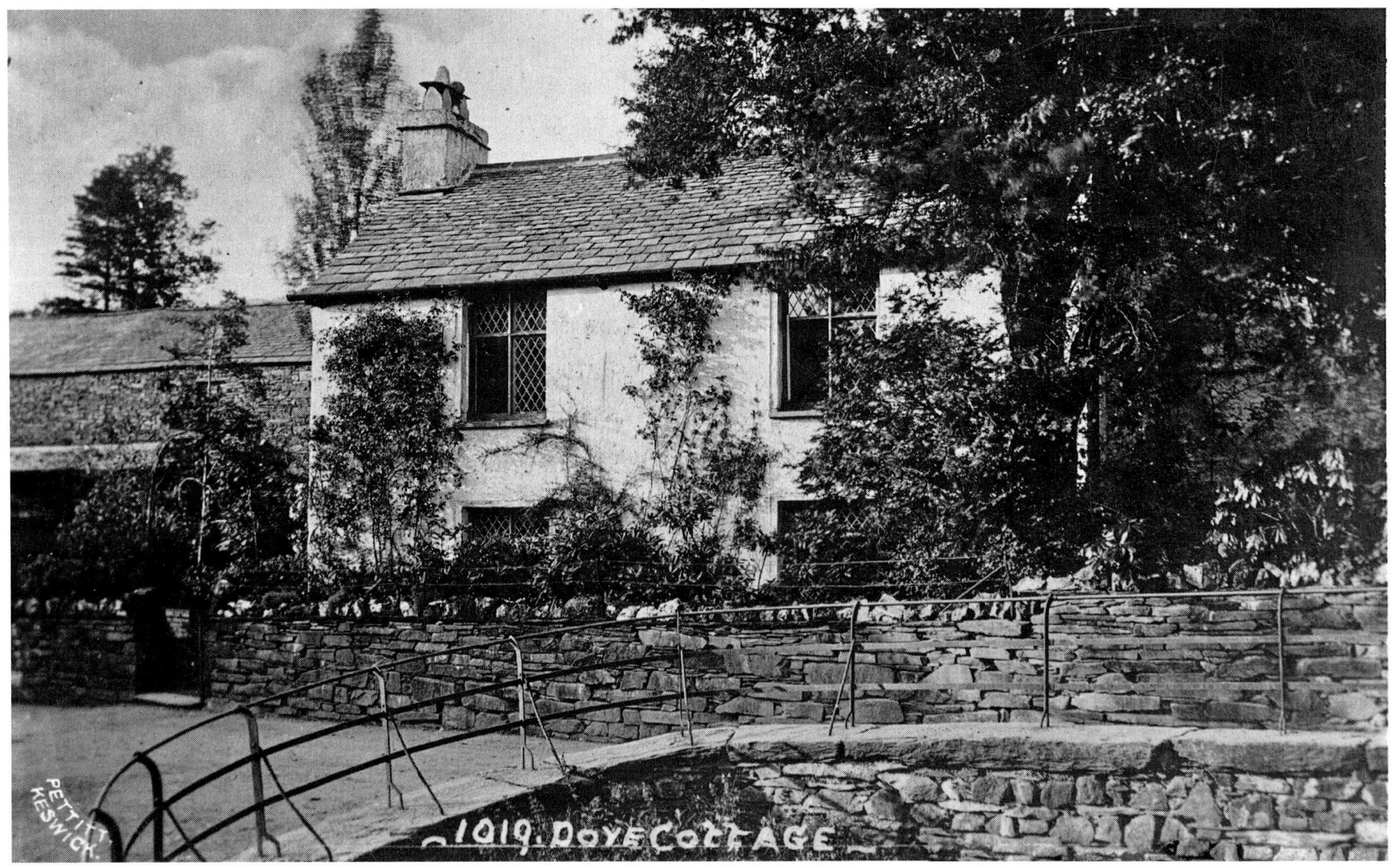

Dove Cottage was the small dwelling rented between 1799 and 1808 by the Lakeland poet William Wordsworth and his sister Dorothy. The cottage had been built in the early seventeenth century as an inn, the "Dove and Olive", but closed in 1793. At Dove Cottage, the poet enjoyed eight years of "plain living, but high thinking". There he wrote much of his best work, and there, too, Dorothy wrote her "Journals", a fascinating account of the Lakeland life of the time. This view of Dove Cottage is in Edwardian times, long after Wordsworth had left, showing it still well-preserved. In 1890 the building was purchased for £650 by the Wordsworth Trust, and was opened to the public the following year. Around 70,000 people visit the cottage annually.

6

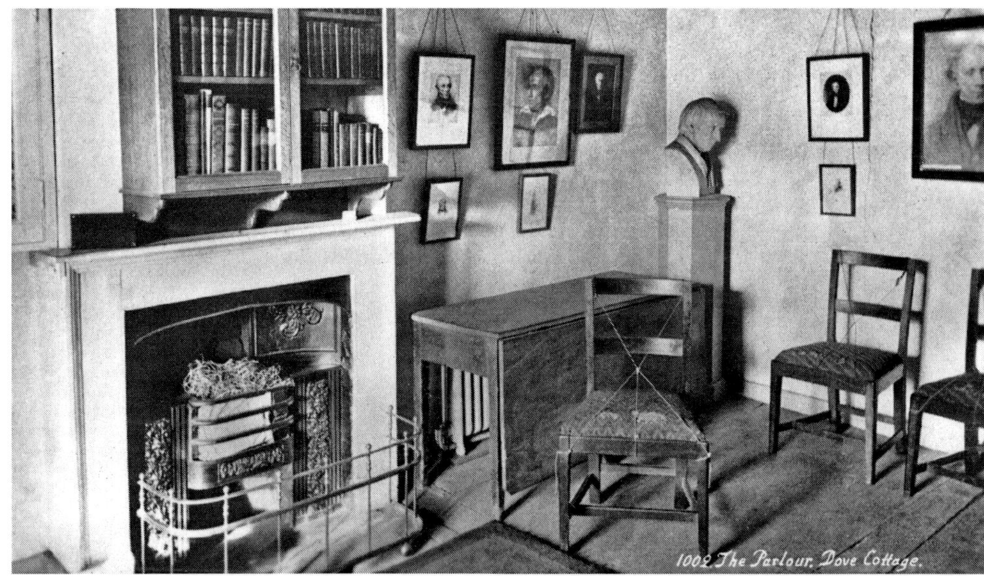

1002 The Parlour, Dove Cottage.

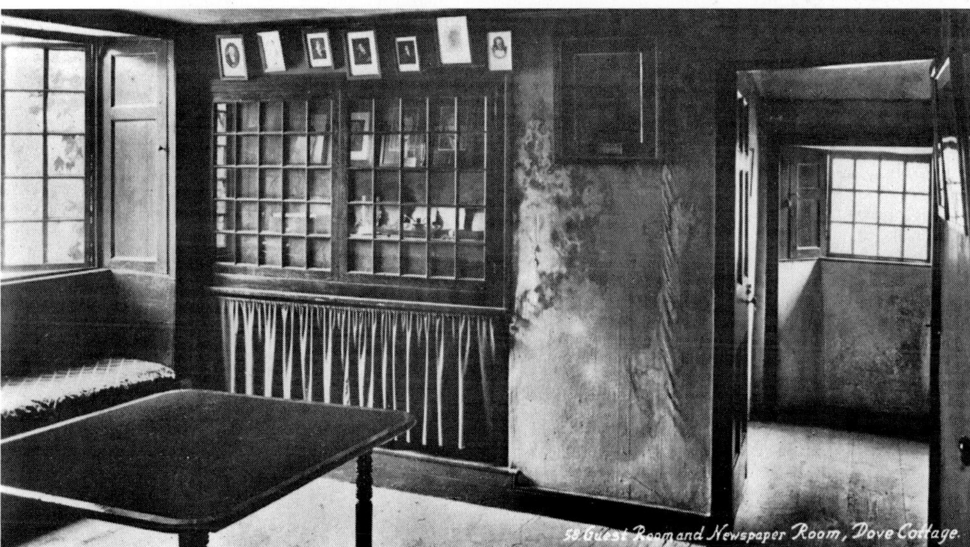

58 Guest Room and Newspaper Room, Dove Cottage.

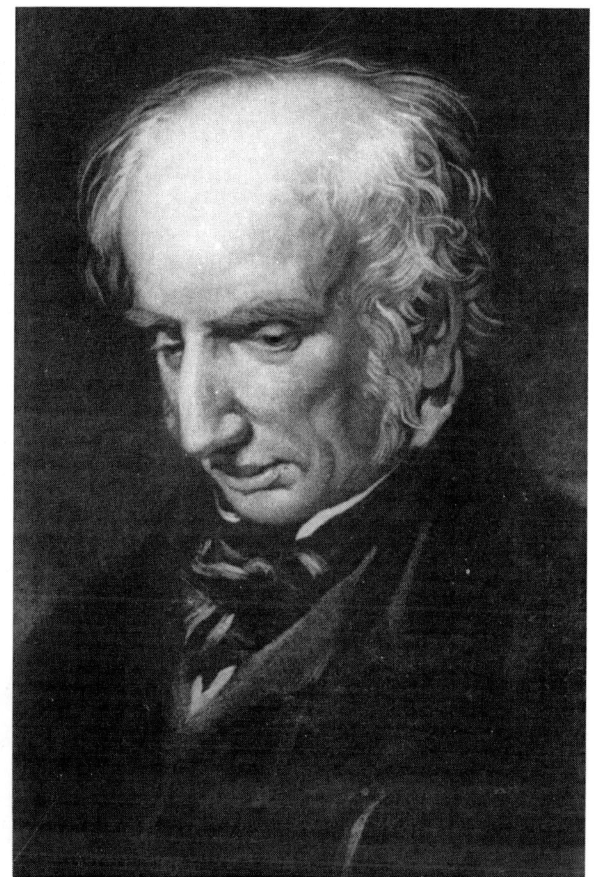

William Wordsworth married his childhood friend Mary Hutchinson in 1802, and three of their children – John, Dora and Thomas – were born at Dove Cottage. Every attempt has been made to preserve Dove Cottage as the famous poet would have known it, and today's visitors may view the kitchen, the bedrooms and the parlour – as these postcards show. The furniture either belonged to the family, or is contemporary with their residence.

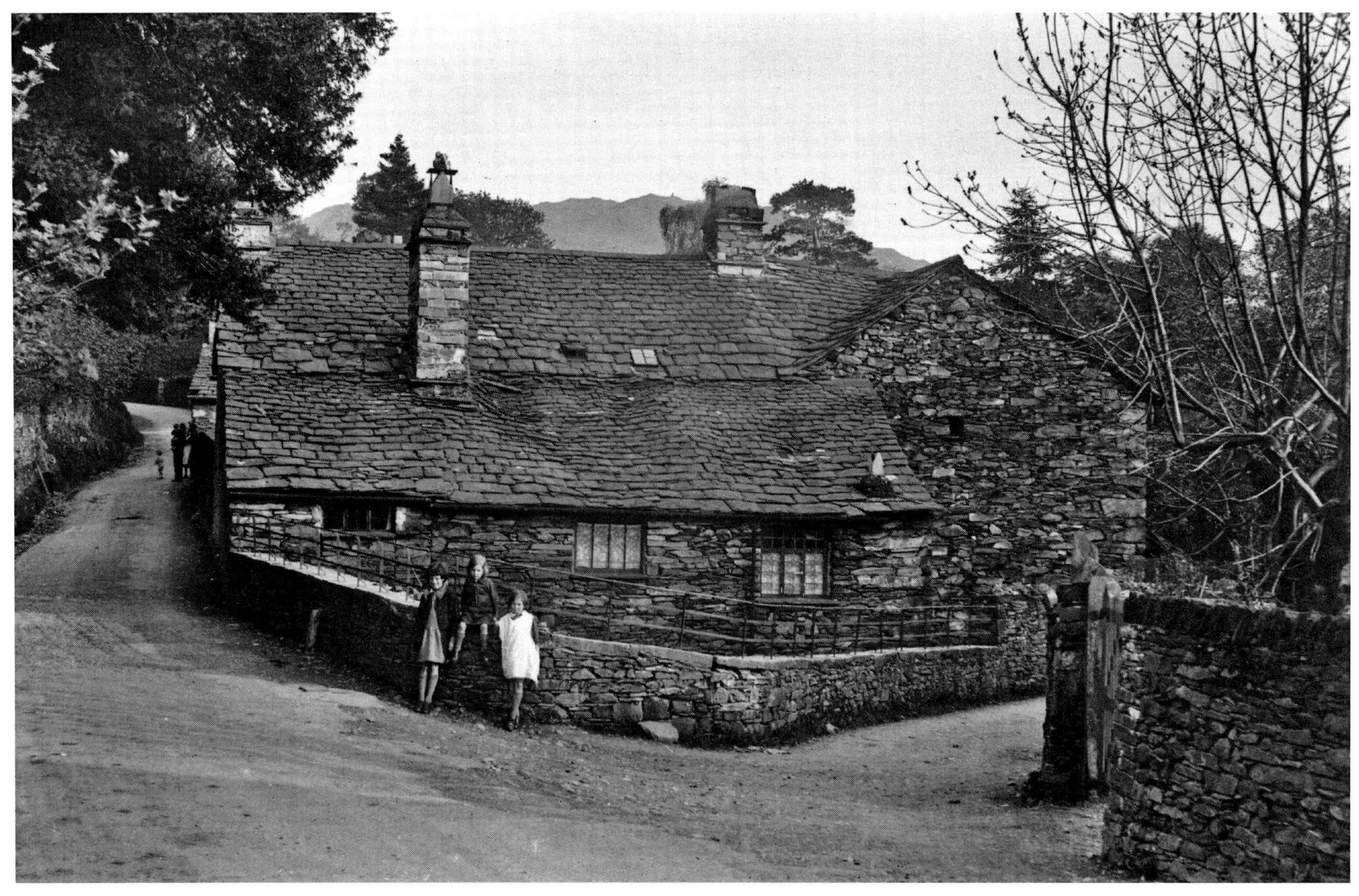

Many of the buildings which originally surrounded Dove Cottage have gone, but this building – Molly Fisher's House – still stands. Molly Fisher was a local girl who was employed as a maid by the Wordsworths at Dove Cottage. This is one of Alan Stephenson's favourite postcards, as the taller girl standing on the left is his mother!

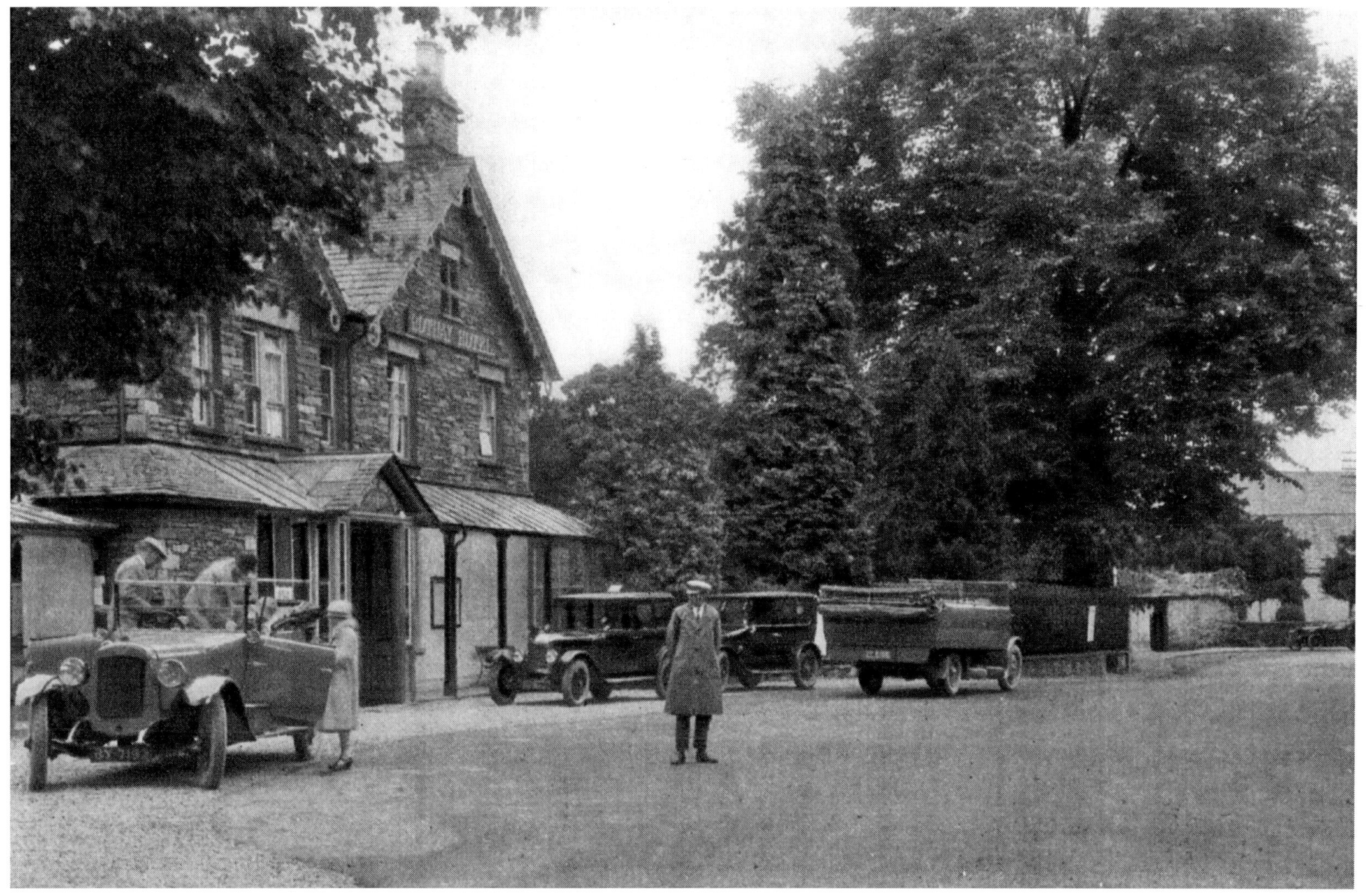

Grasmere is not large – the population today is less than a thousand – but during the season large numbers of tourists flock to the village just for a visit, or to stay in one of the many hotels, B&Bs or hostels in the area. This postcard, perhaps dating from the early 1930s, shows a group of cars and charabancs outside the Rothay Hotel, close to the centre of the village.

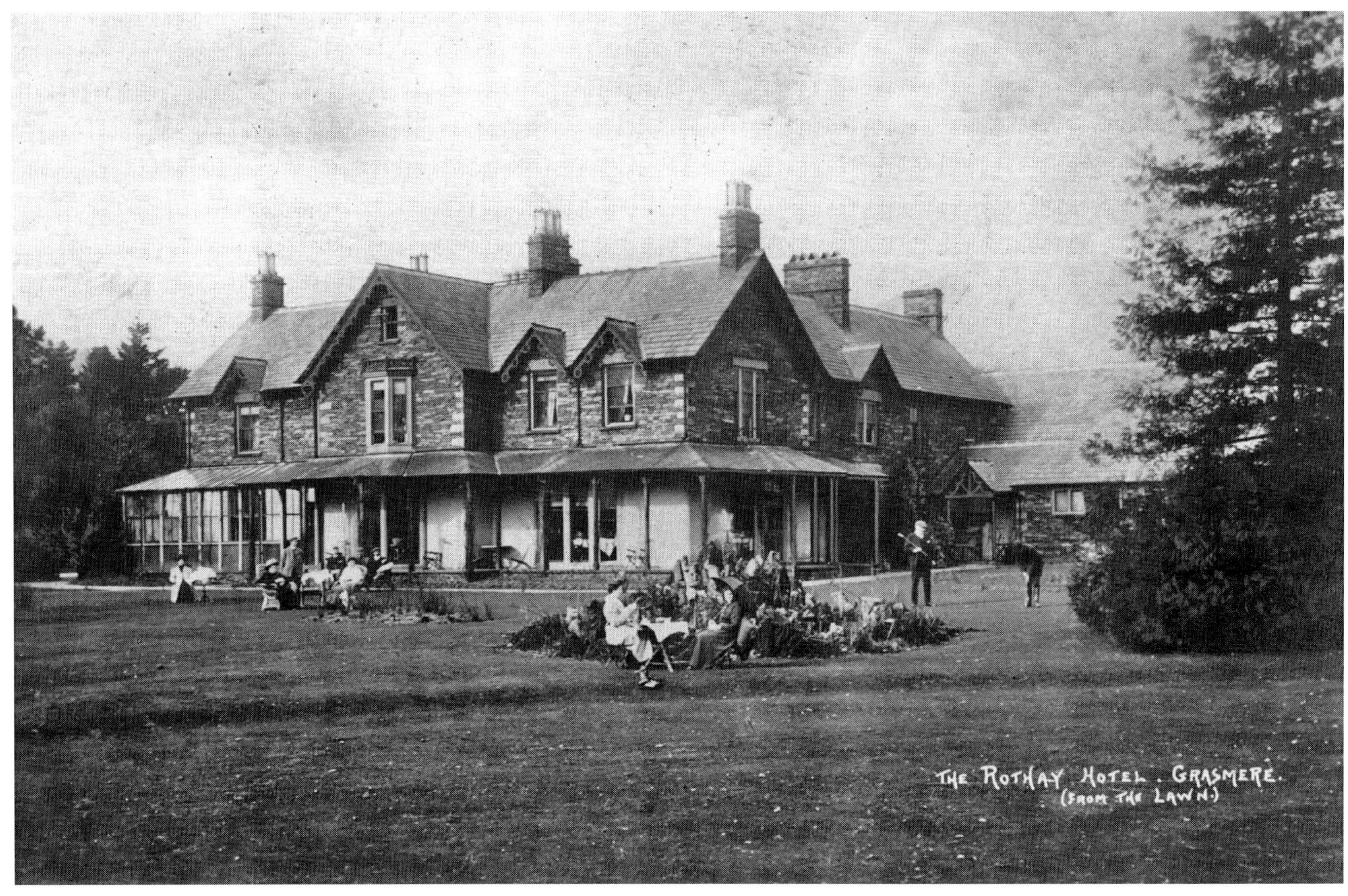

This postcard shows another view of the Rothay Hotel, which was built by the Earl of Cadogan. The hotel is viewed from the rear lawns, where a number of the guests may be seen enjoying afternoon tea. The hotel advertised its own tennis courts, nine-hole putting green and private trout fishing, as well as its "irreproachable cuisine".

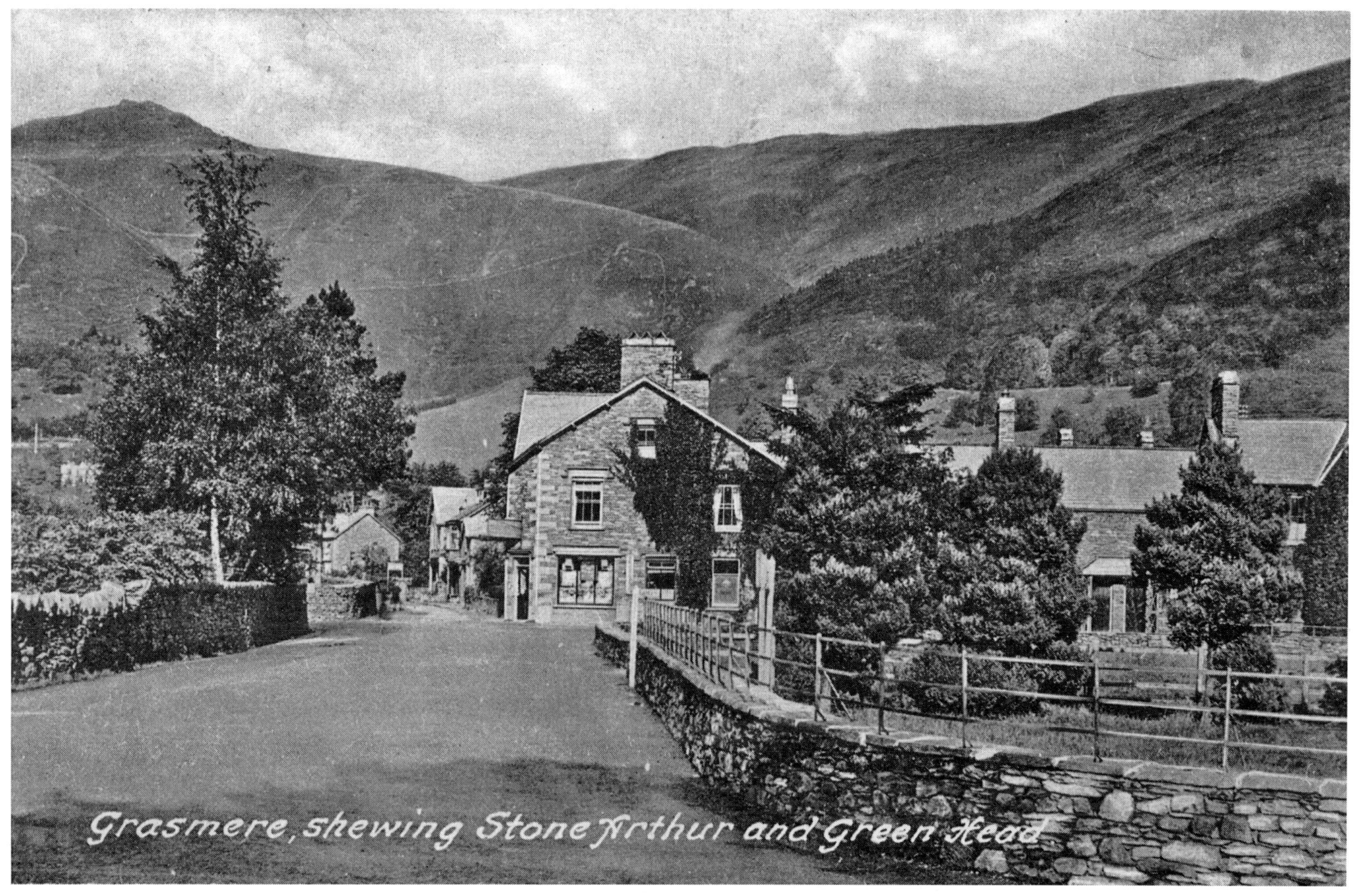

This 1920s postcard shows a view of Broadgate, with its cluster of corner shops, including an ironmonger's, a cycle agent and a boot repairer. Stone Arthur, rising to the left in the background, boasts the only reference to the mythical king in the area. The fell is at the eastern end of the Fairfield Horseshoe, a popular walkers' route, and from a distance its summit resembles the walls of a ruined castle.

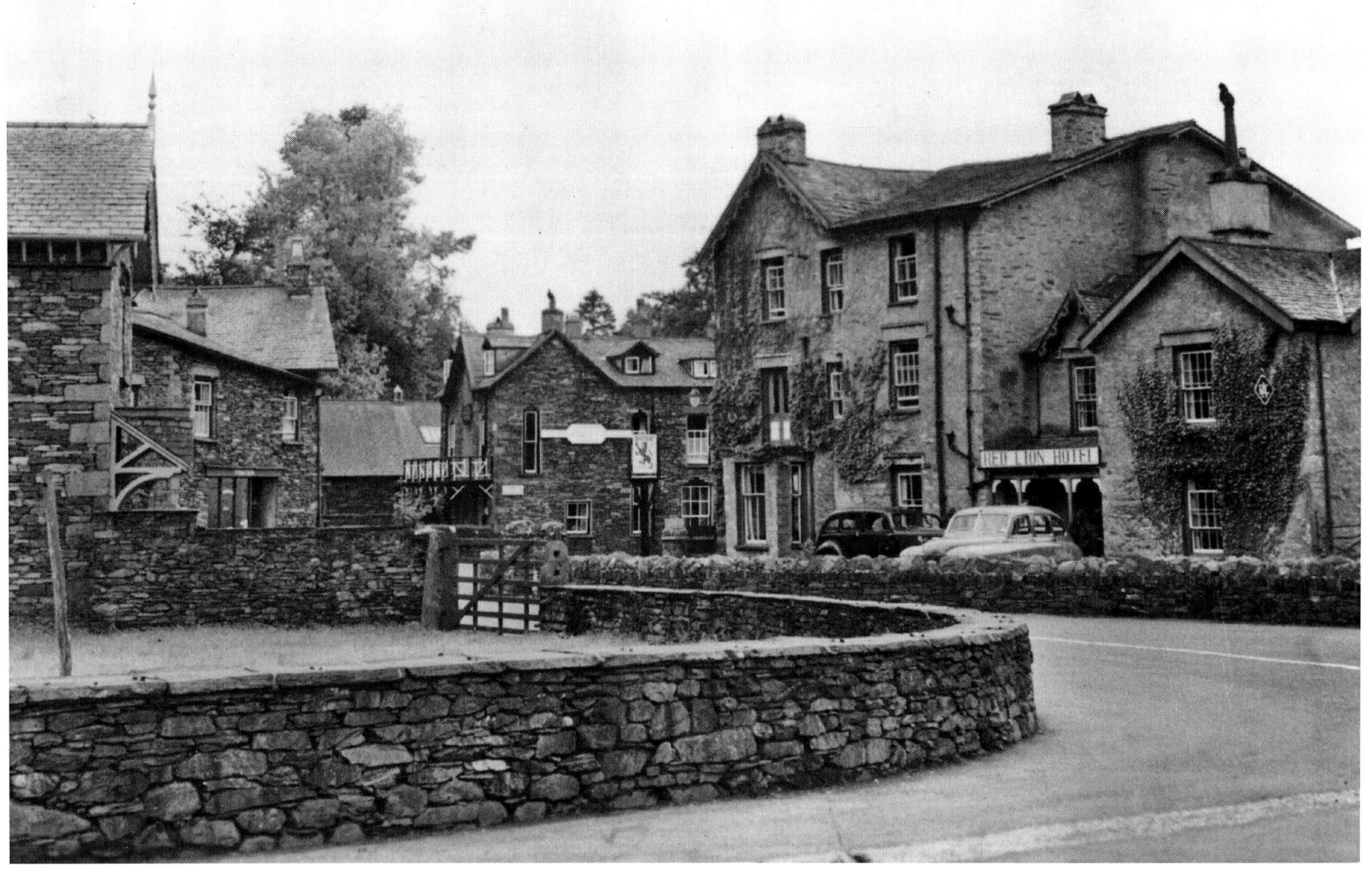

Situated in the centre of Grasmere, the Red Lion Hotel was originally a coaching inn and it has given its name to the main square in the village. Grasmere's pubs have all disappeared, though part of this hotel is still known as a "pub". In the early twentieth century, in common with the other large hotels in the area, the Red Lion always advertised that it was A.A. appointed and had a garage – no mention of hikers!

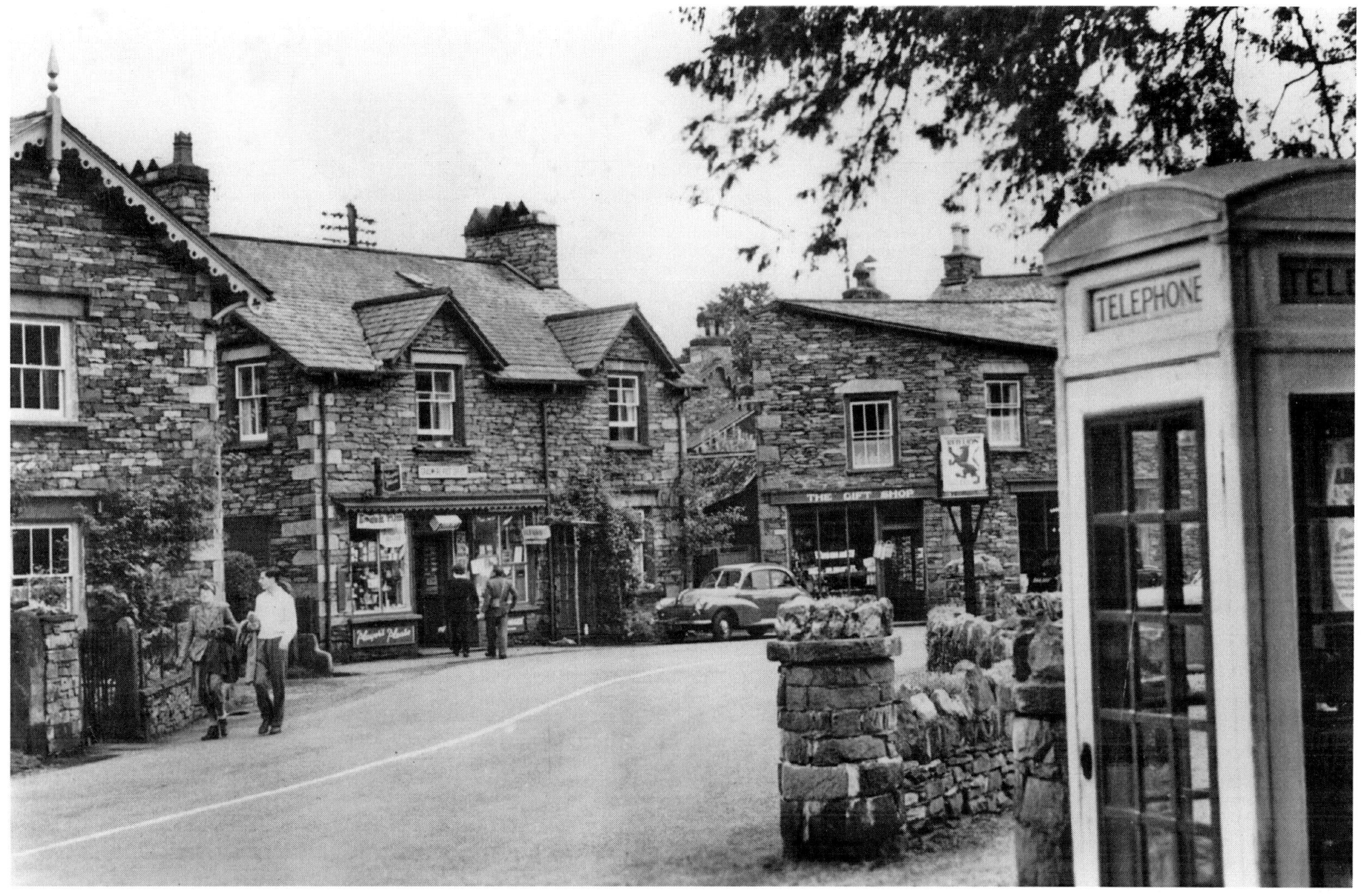

This post-war view shows the heart of Grasmere village just before car ownership transformed the Lake District. Note the old-style red telephone box, the "Red Lion" sign, Grasmere Post Office and *The* Gift Shop, and just one car and a few tourists – there would surely be much more activity than this today, even on a wet weekday in the depths of winter!

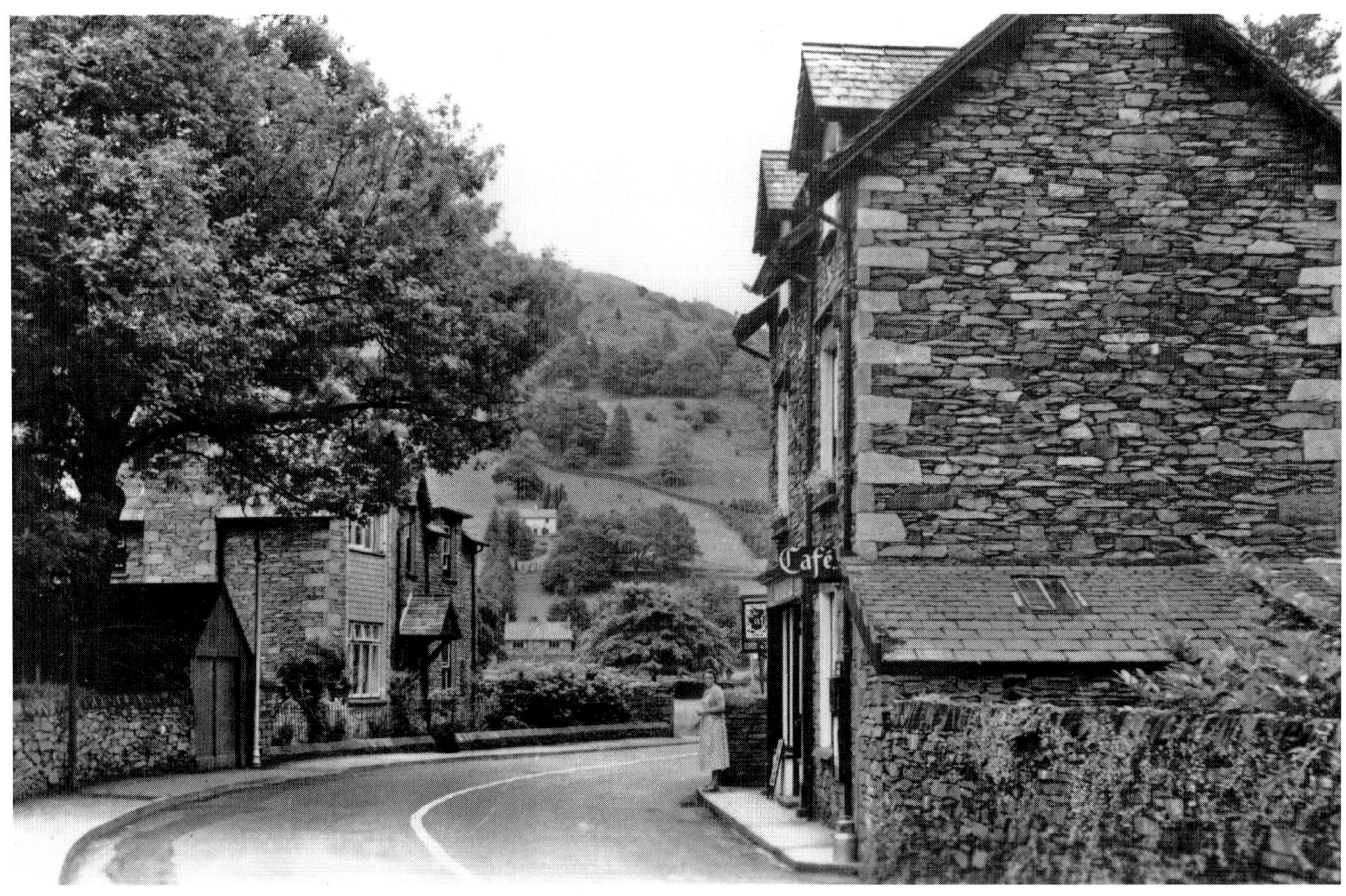

The previous page mentions *The* Gift Shop and this postcard shows *The* Little Café, suggesting that they were the only ones open at that time, probably just after the Second World War. How times have changed! Nowadays there is a wide choice of cafes and gift shops to attract the hordes of tourists who visit the village every year.

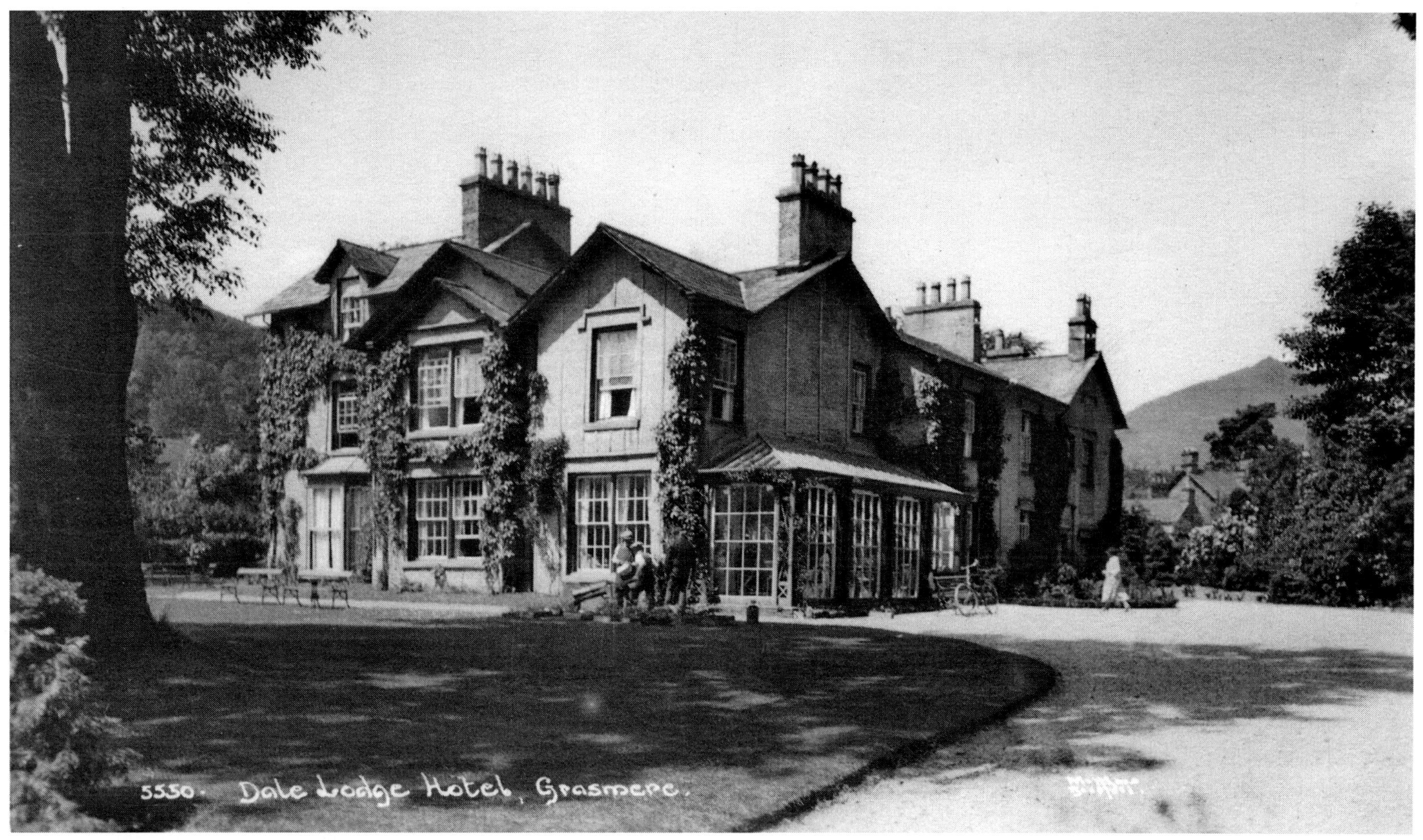

A 1931 brochure describes this hotel thus: "A delightful mansion standing in its own attractive grounds. Specially adapted to the requirements of those who prefer an unlicensed Hotel with home comforts, pleasant company, first class food and efficient service. Within easy walking distance of the Lake. Garage." The cost for a day's stay in this utopia, including room, bath, breakfast, luncheon, afternoon tea and dinner – but no beer! – was just fifteen shillings. There were also many bed & breakfast establishments available to tourists in the 1930s. The detached residence Laurel Villa offered views of Helm Crag and Silverhow, and its proprietress, Mrs Preston, stressed that the property boasted "modern conveniences", such as a bath, hot and cold running water, and electric light! A rival B&B, Brimmer Head Farmhouse at Easedale, was eager to advertise that it was an excellent centre for climbers and walkers, and that it had "indoor sanitation"!

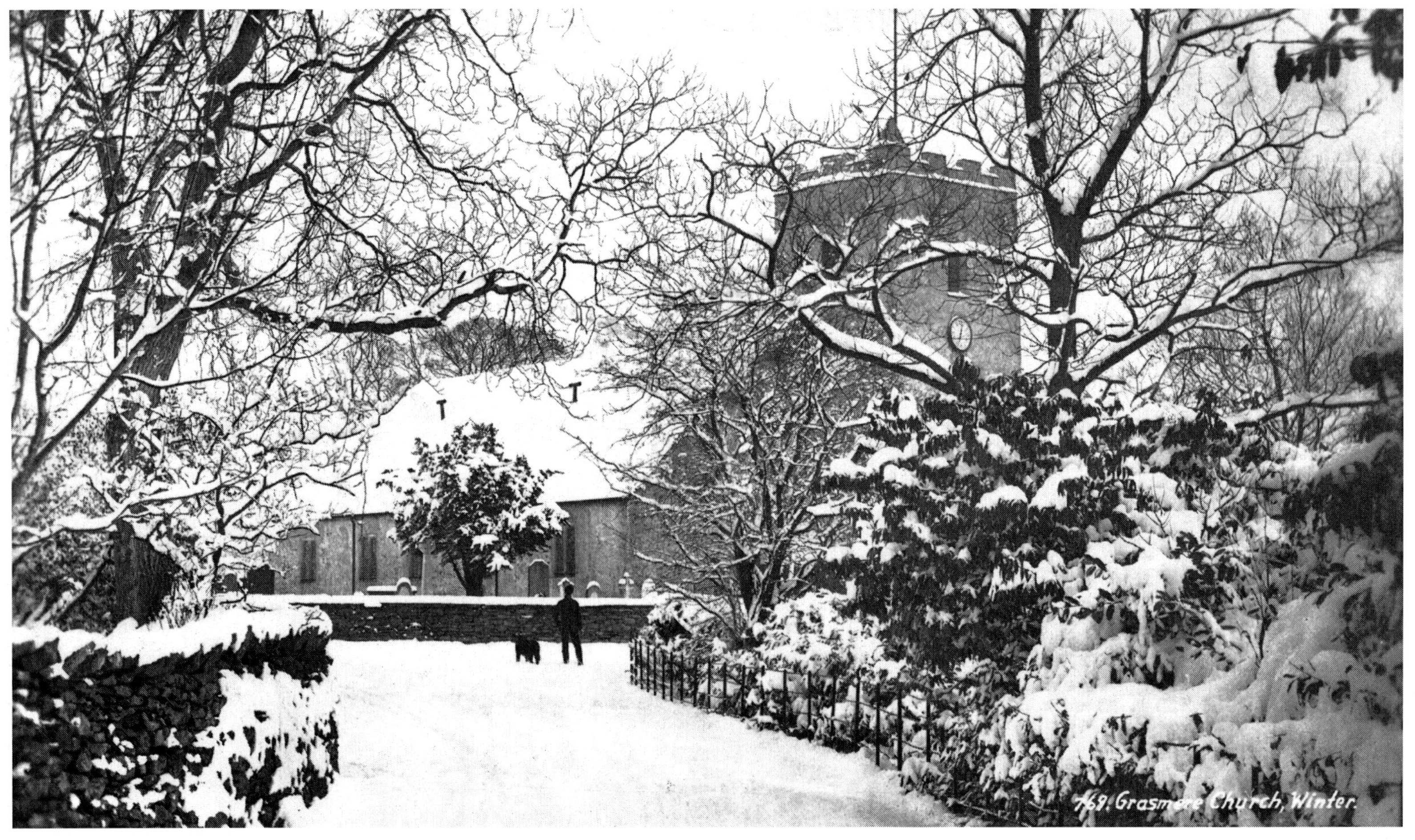

It is thought that the saintly King Oswald of Northumbria preached in the Grasmere area, and that a small wooden church was built there around 642. The present church, dedicated to the saint, dates from the fourteenth century and was extended in the fifteenth century and restored in 1840. The church is constructed from roughcast stone and has a slate roof. It has a double nave and a south-eastern tower, which was battered (i.e. with the lower walls sloping out), perhaps as protection against marauding reivers. The twelve graves enclosed by iron railings in the churchyard are probably the most visited "literary" graves outside those in Westminster Abbey. The central grave is that of William Wordsworth and his wife Mary, and it is surrounded by those of their children (Catherine, Dora, Thomas and William), Dora's husband Edward Quillanin, Wordsworth's sister Dorothy, his sister-in-law Sara Hutchinson and Hartley Coleridge. Wordsworth planted twelve yew trees in the churchyard, and one of them guards his family's graves.

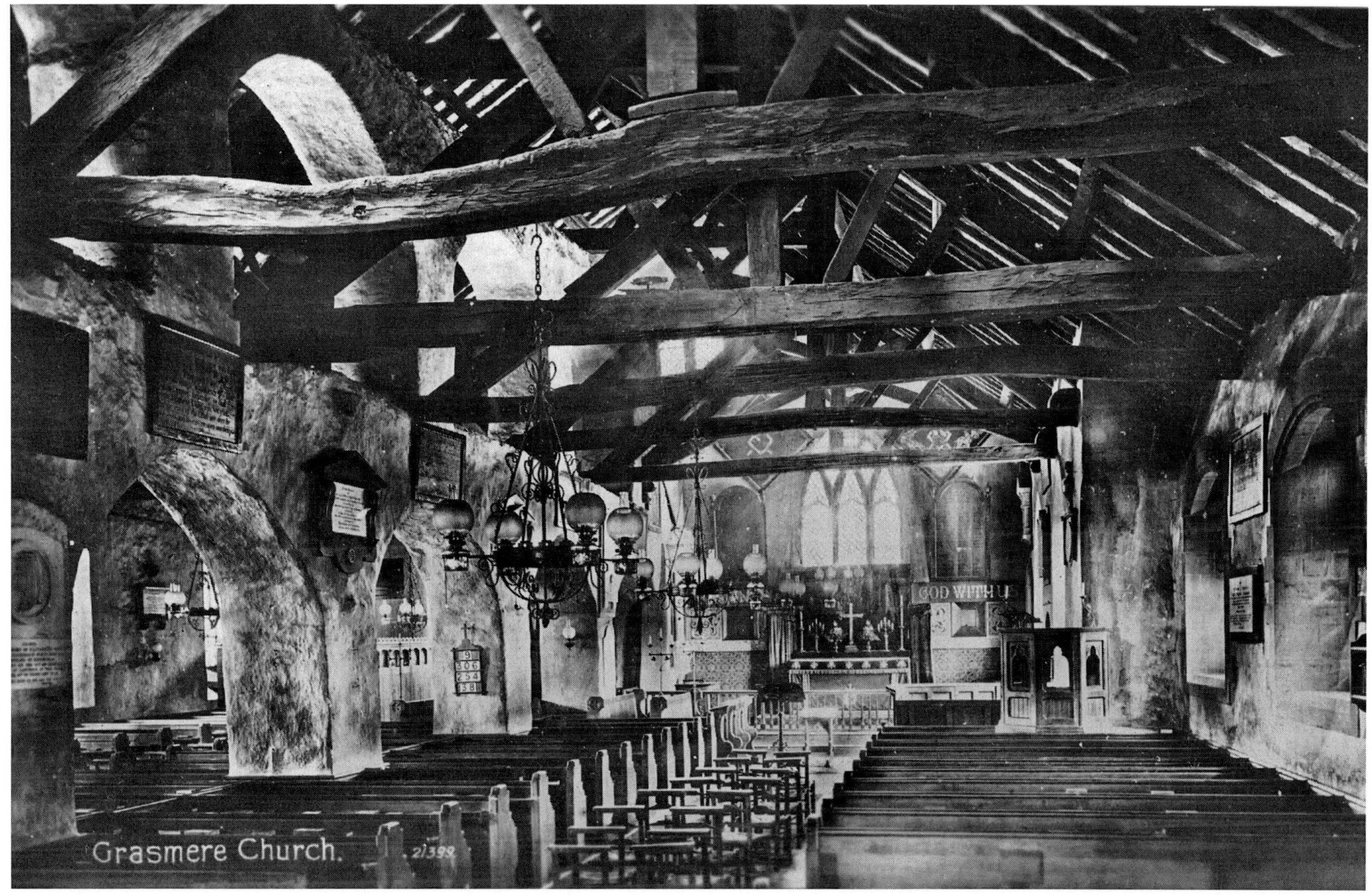

There is little of remark within the church. It has a medieval font, and some stained glass dating from medieval times, but most of the furnishings are more modern. The oak pews date from 1881. There are several memorials inside the nave, the most impressive belonging to the le Fleming family, who lived at nearby Rydal Hall. Look at the twisted cross-beams!

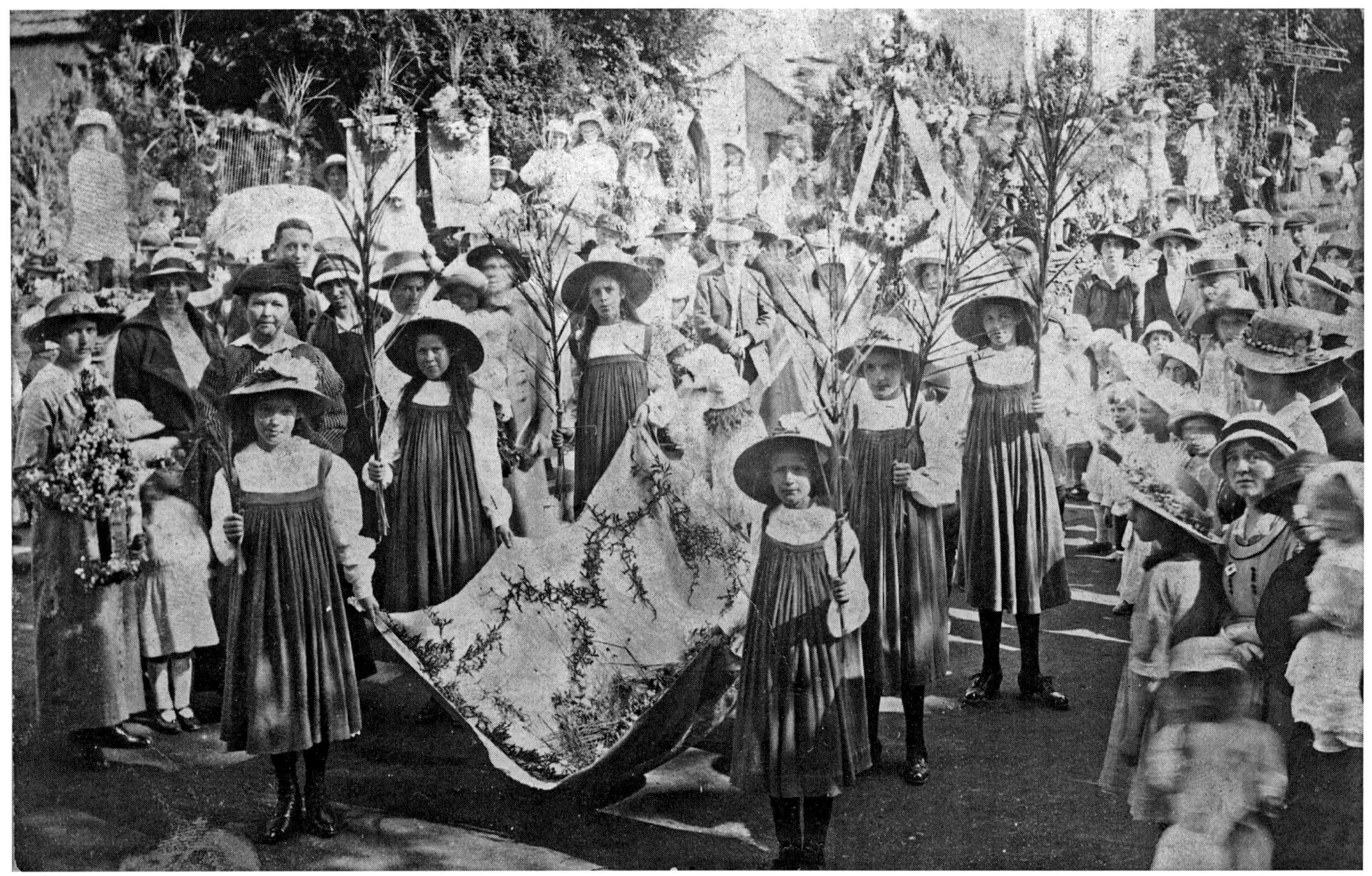

In pre-Reformation times the floors of churches were of beaten earth, and rushes were generally used as a floor-covering. As the practice of nave burials ceased, stone or wooden floors became more common, and the need for rushes or rushbearing declined. In some places, mainly in the north, festivals were associated with the patron saint of the church, and in Grasmere rushbearing survived the laying of the church floor around 1840. After the festival, there was a dance in a barn near the Red Lion Hotel, and wrestling took place in the adjoining field.

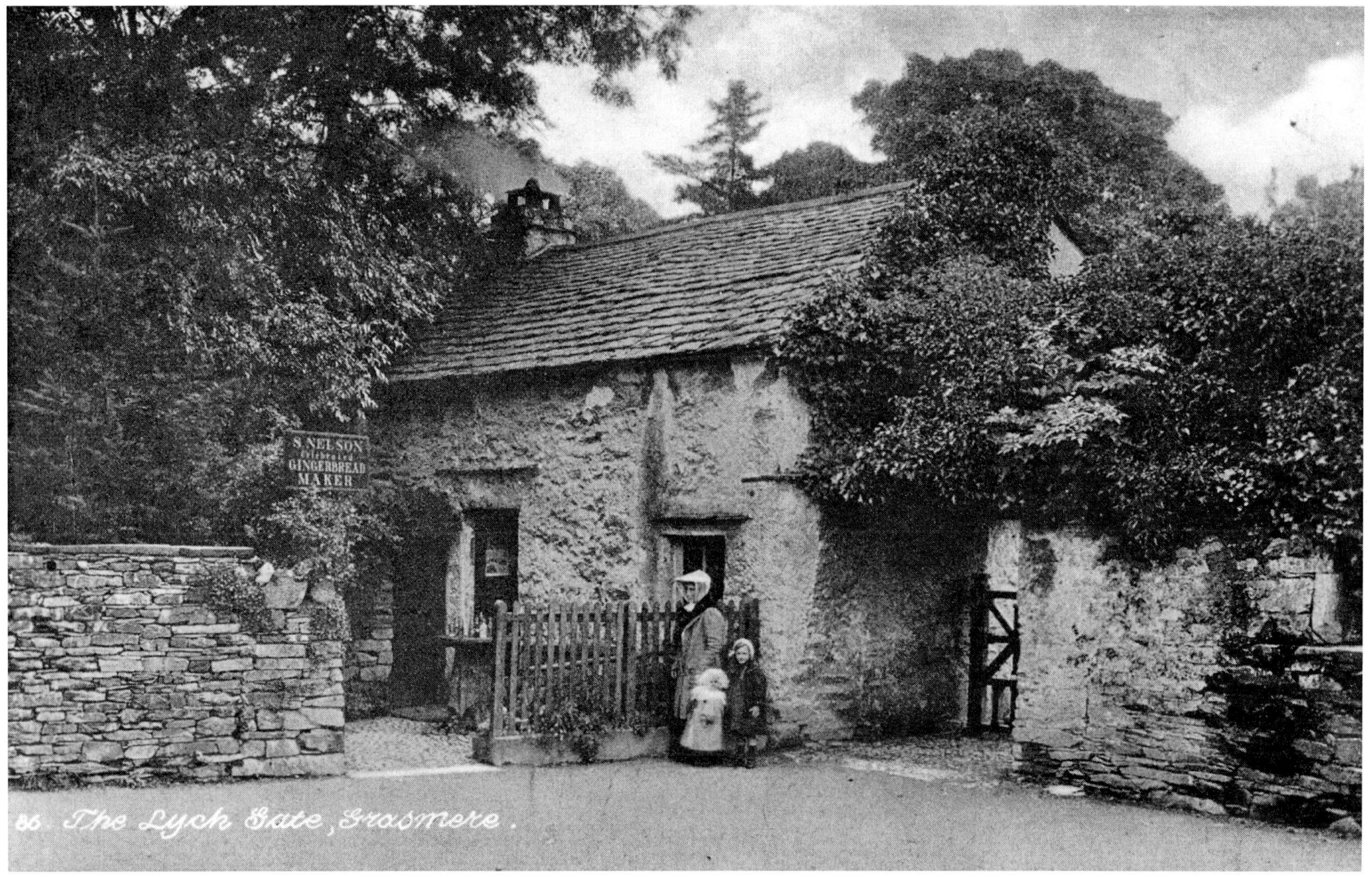

One of Grasmere's celebrated attractions was, and still is, Sarah Nelson's Gingerbread Shop, which was established in a small cottage by the lych gate at the northern side of the churchyard. Church Cottage, built in the seventeenth century, had been used as the village school in Victorian times. Sarah developed a new recipe for her gingerbread, which she baked daily and sold to customers outside her cottage. Her husband, Wilfred, was the local gravedigger, and both are buried in the nearby churchyard.

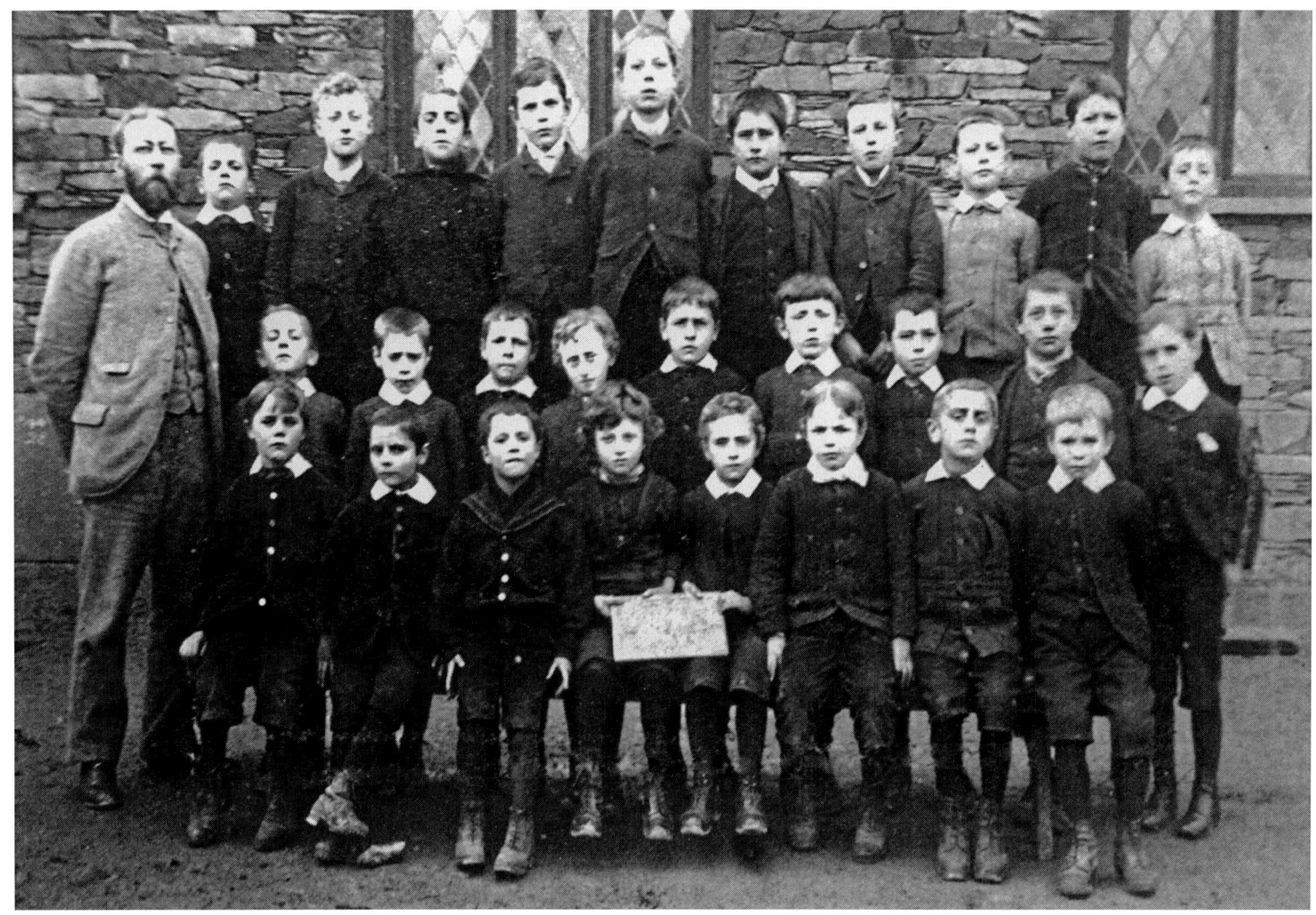

This Victorian photo shows a group of local children at Grasmere, all dressed in their "Sunday best" for Sunday School. The strict-looking gentleman on the left is William Fuller, Alan Stephenson's great-great-grandfather. He had a fearsome reputation, and as well as being the local teacher, he took Sunday School and was church organist for over forty years!

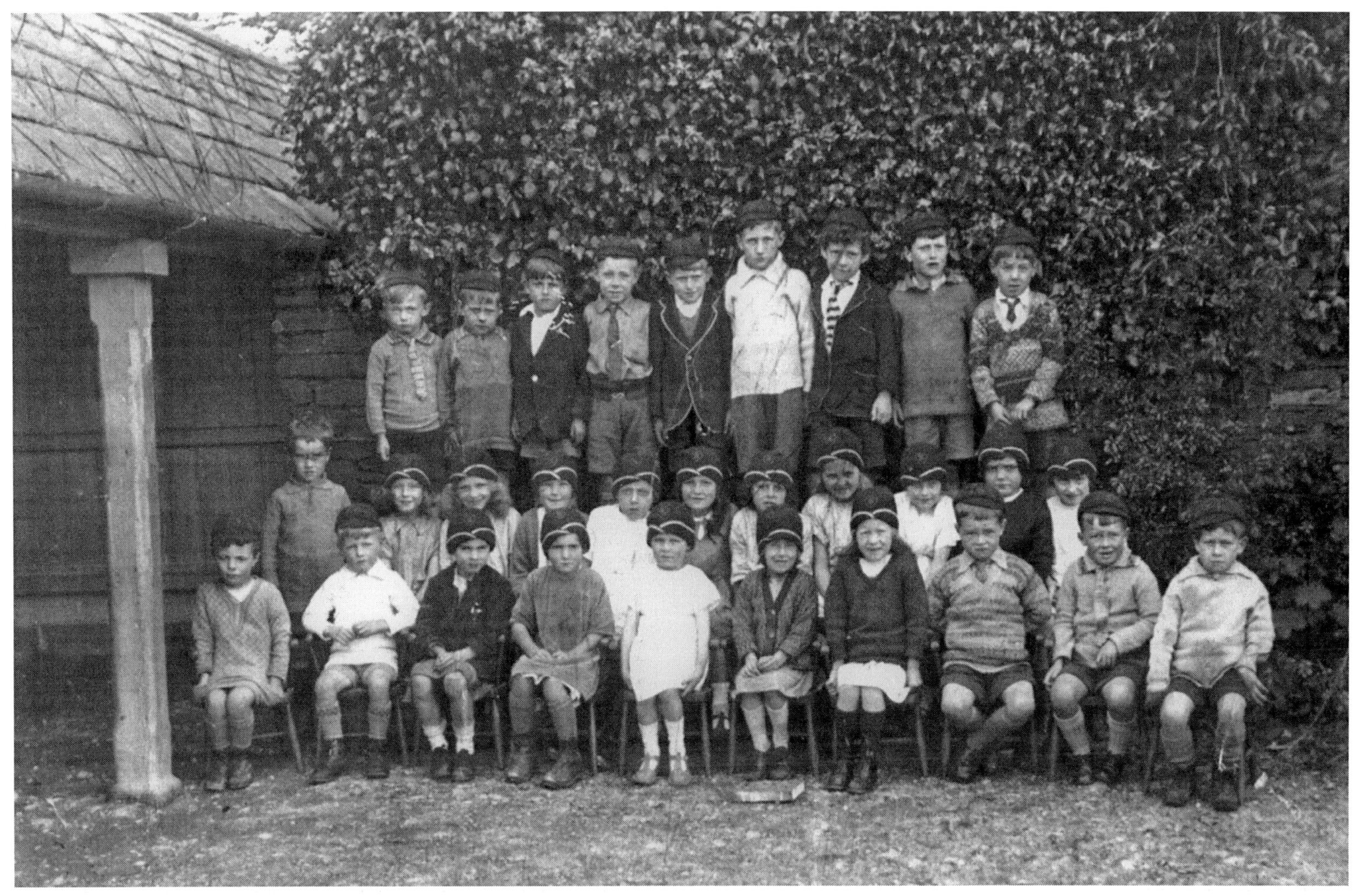

In contrast to the previous photo, these children would appear to have more in common with the Bash Street Kids, than with a sleepy Lakeland school! The photo was taken around 1930, and it suggests firstly that many of the village families were quite poor, and secondly that a school uniform was not considered to be very important!

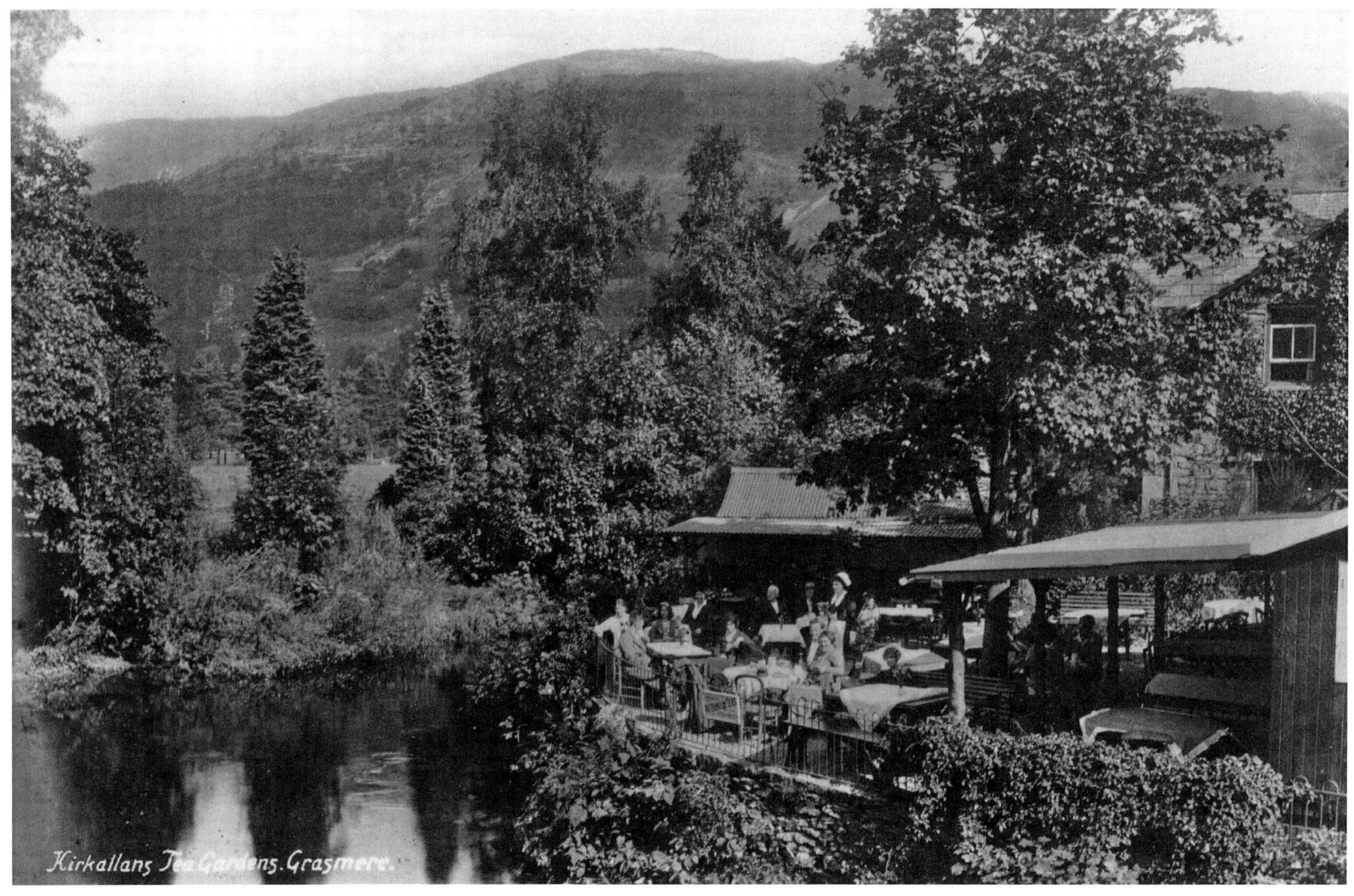

The Grasmere Tea Gardens were established on the bank of the River Rothay, but this postcard does not show us the splendid view of St. Oswald's Church across the river. The sender of this postcard writes: "…..the weather yesterday was grand. Climbed Wansfell Pike in the morning and went to Grasmere in the afternoon. Had tea in the gardens shown on this card."

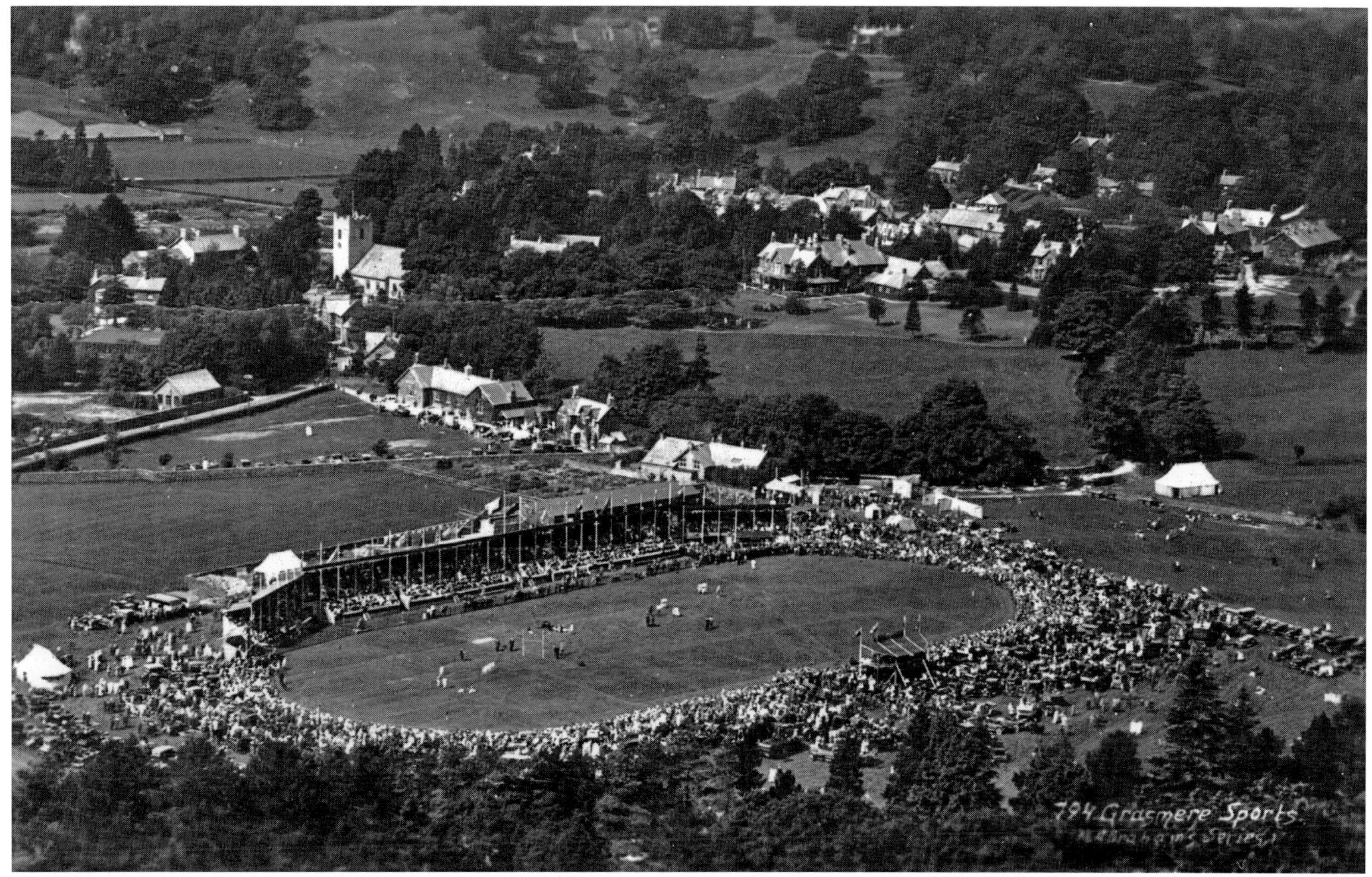

The world-famous Grasmere Sports are held each year on the Thursday nearest to the 20th August. This elevated view, dating from around 1910, shows the grandstands and crowds which surrounded the sports field. The earliest surviving records of the sports are from 1852, but their origins lay in the wrestling competitions which took place on the village green on the evening following the Rushbearing celebrations. Gradually, other "old-time" sports were added – the guides race for fell-runners, pole-leaping and hound trailing. Most of these sports were distinctly Lakeland in character.

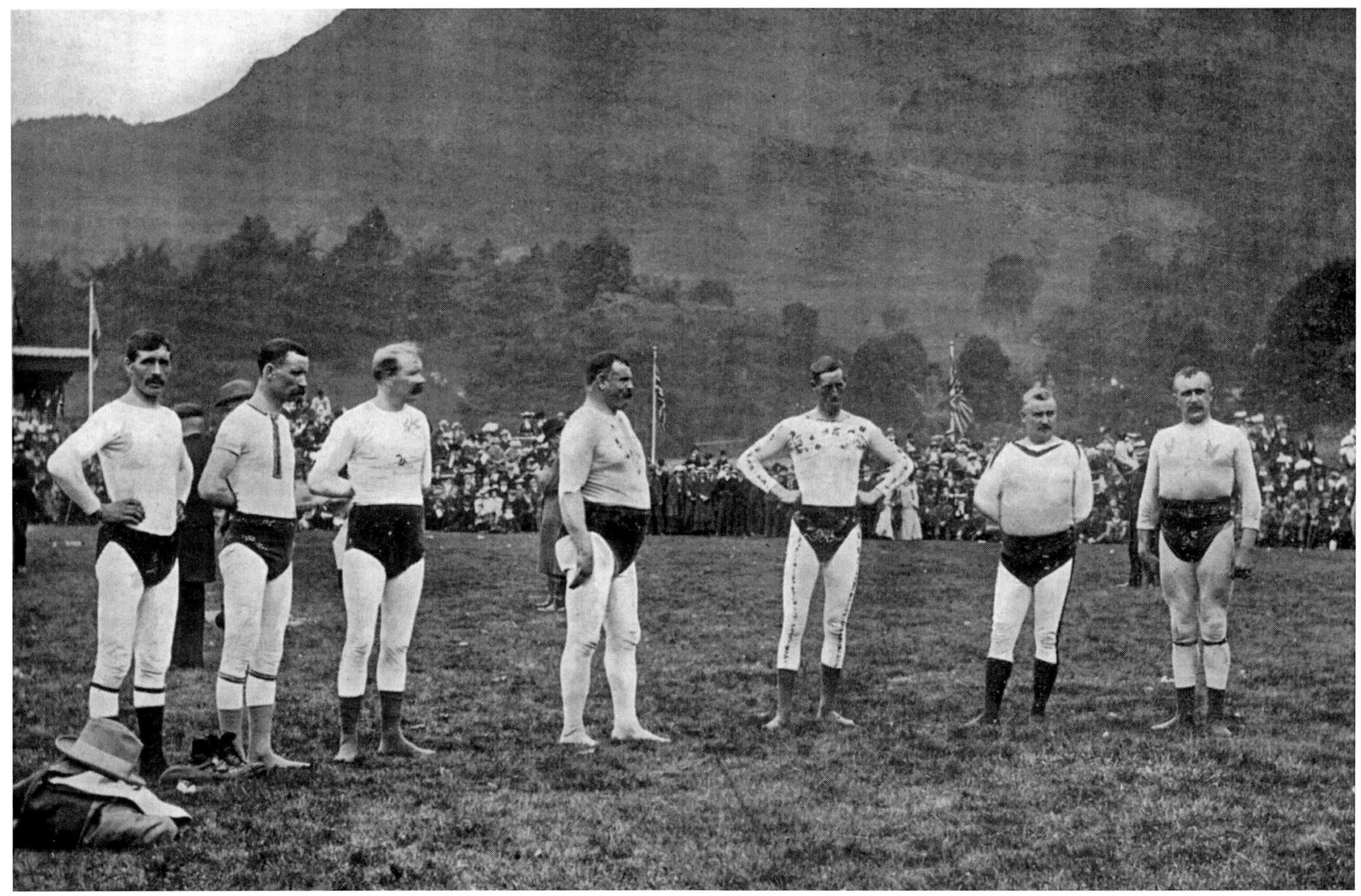

This photo shows a group of celebrated wrestlers in 1903. Cumberland and Westmorland-style wrestling differed considerably from the wrestling featured on TV today. At Grasmere, pairs of wrestlers gripped each other behind the back, and attempted to "fall" their opponents by making them lose their grip or footing. The colourful pants, worn Superman-style outside the tights, were judged in a separate competition!

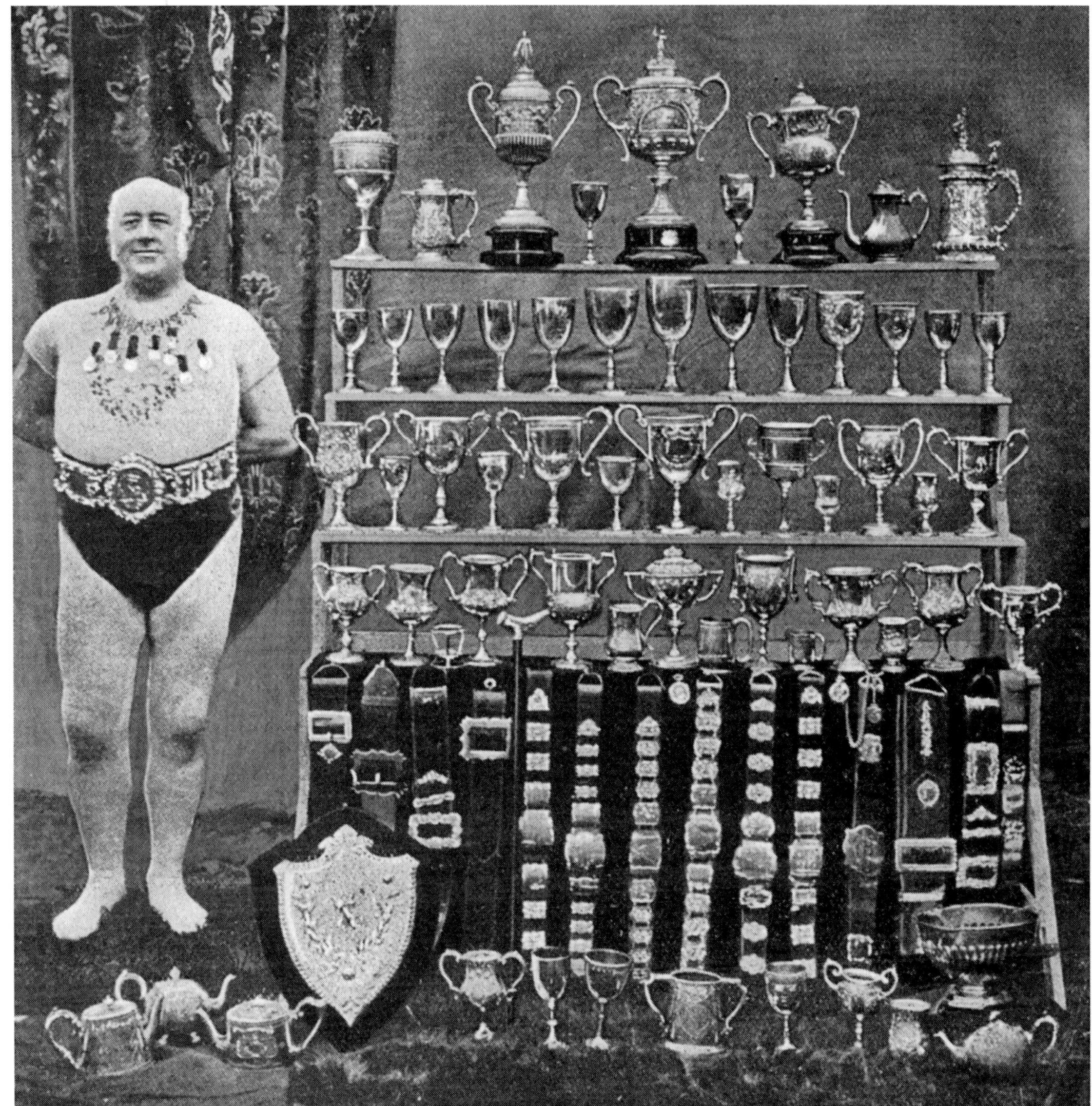

The celebrated wrestler George Steadman, posing alongside part of his "trophy cabinet". During a career of over 30 years, Steadman won over 60 cups, 20 belts, heaps of medals and more prize money than any contemporary. He was champion wrestler at Grasmere 17 times, but he also excelled at other forms of wrestling, winning several foreign competitions. One of his most famous victories was against Matt Hall, the "Lancashire Giant", who, though over 6ft 7in tall and weighing 23 stone, had such a rough time against Steadman that he was never able again to take part in wrestling competitions! Steadman last fought at Grasmere in 1900, and died four years later at the age of 58.

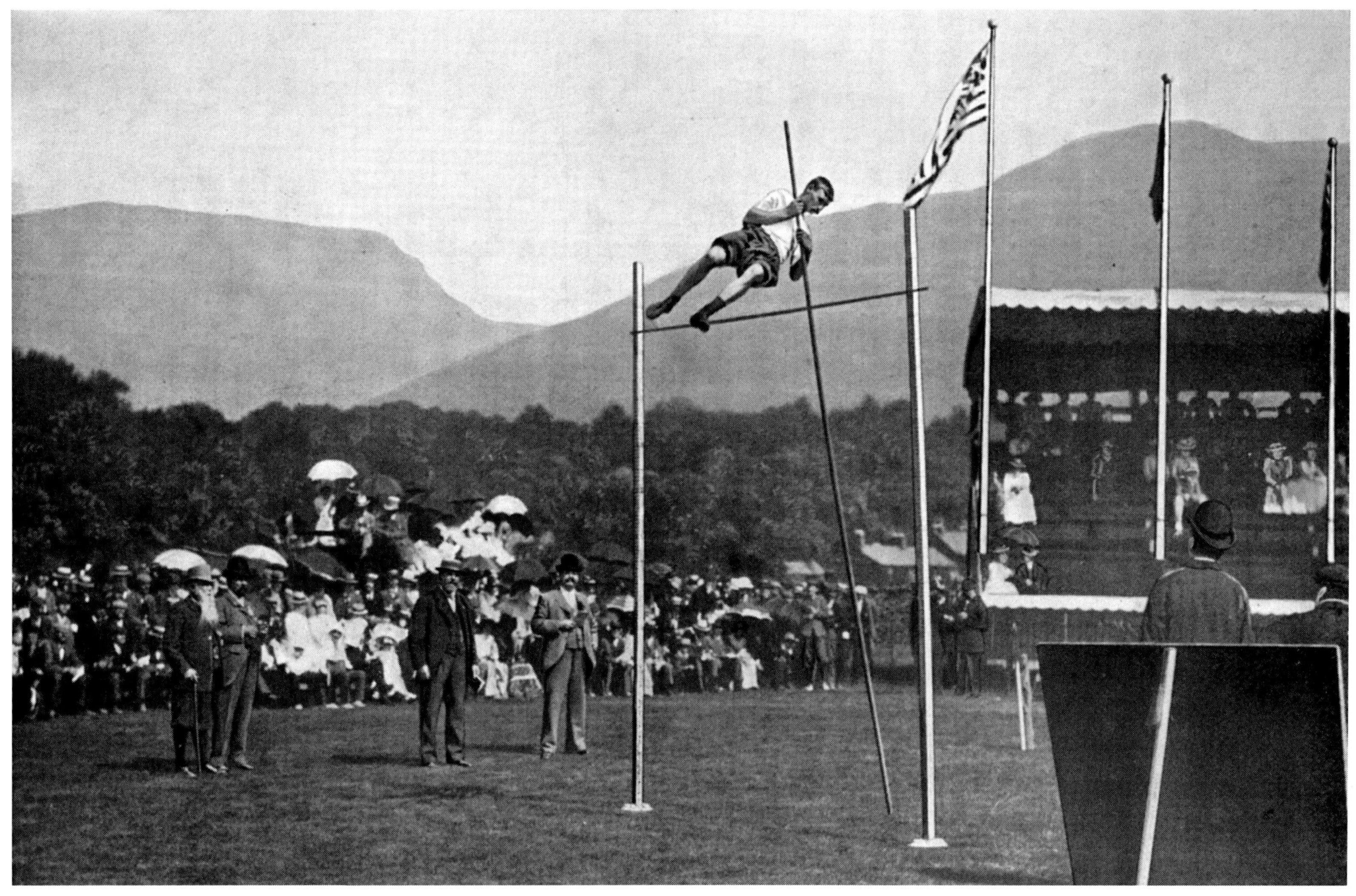

Pole leaping, or pole vaulting as the sport is better-known today, was another popular sport at Grasmere. The heights achieved by the athletes were modest by today's standards, but injuries must have been commonplace, for there were no soft pits to land on and the leapers lacked cushioned shoes, and in some cases, socks!

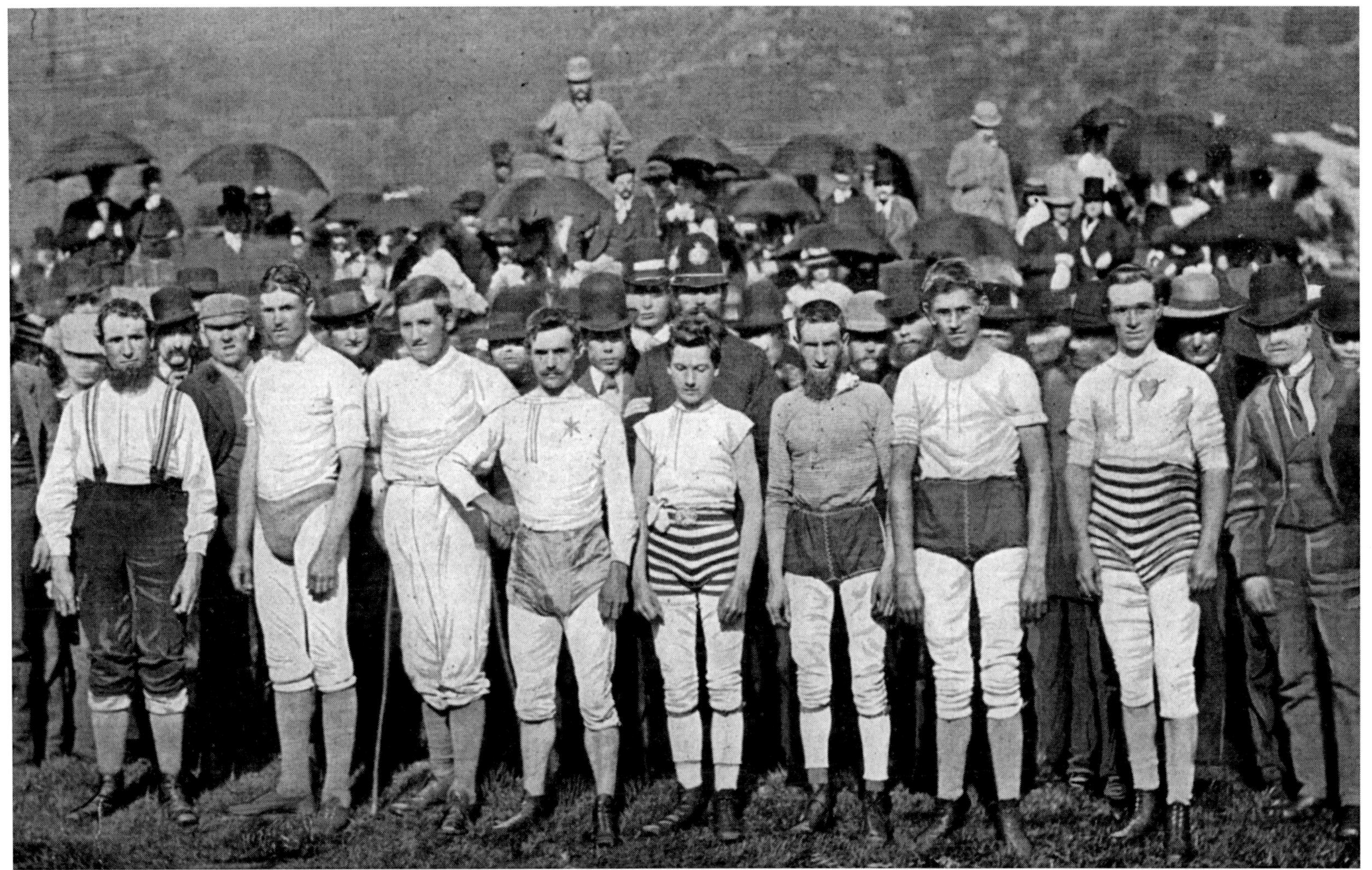

The early sports featured sack races and steeplechases, but the one running event which has continued is the fell race. This was originally called the guides race, and was perhaps limited to those runners who prepared the trails for the hounds, though I have heard that in some parts of the Lake District, the guides were those who guided genteel visitors to a local viewpoint, or summit. They apparently raced naked in the early sports! The photograph suggests that that there was a separate fancy dress prize for the contestants!

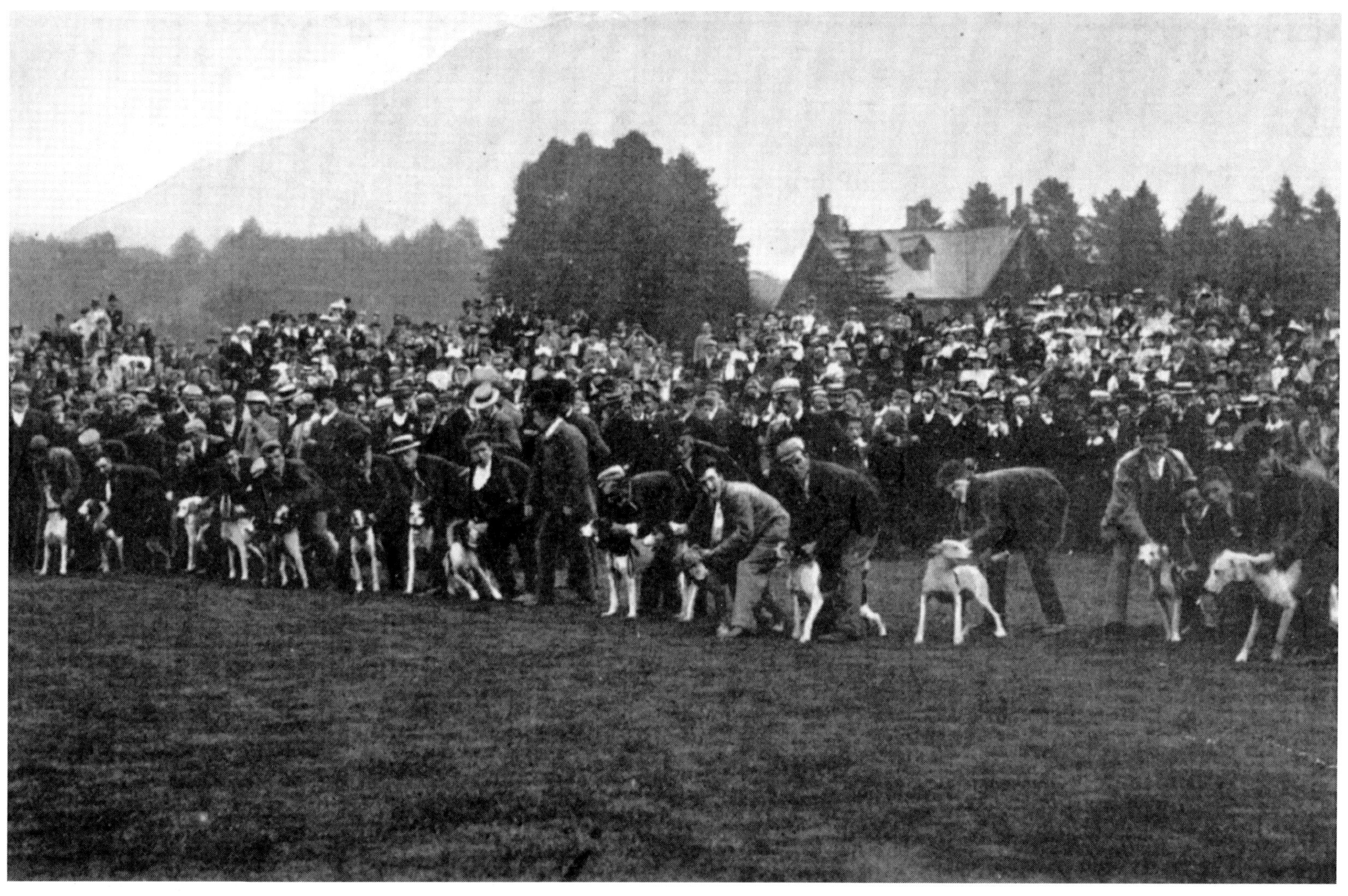

The hound trail began with the release of the competing dogs from the sports field to run over a course which was often 12 miles or more. The trail would be laid by one of the guides dragging a bag of aniseed, and the hounds would have to chase across field and fell, and leap over walls, before returning exhausted to the sports field.

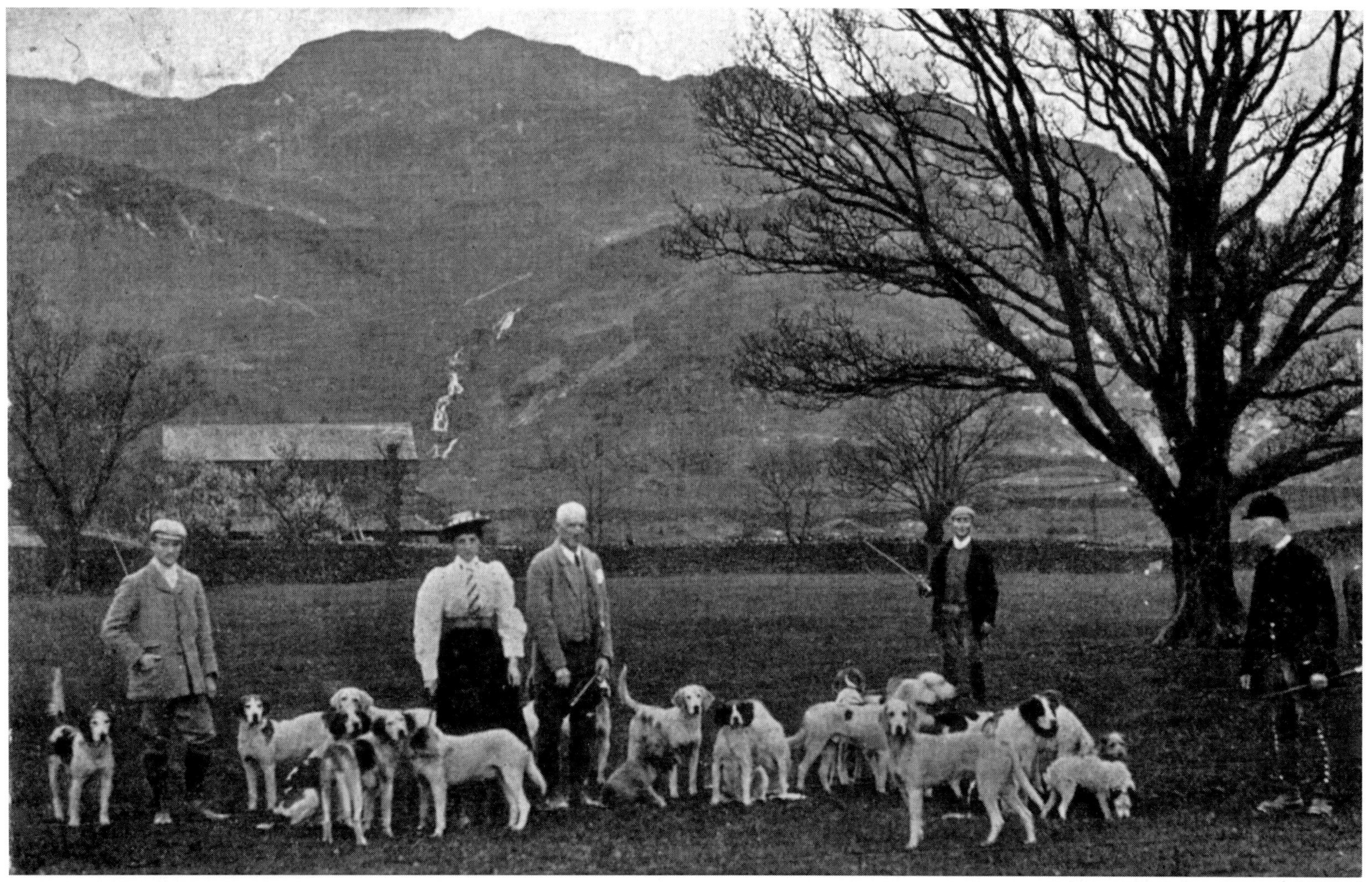

This postcard, posted in 1905, shows the Coniston Fox Hounds at Grasmere, at a time when "Neddie" Reynolds was Master or "Mayor" of the pack. Fox hunting with hounds began in the late 1600s, and the Coniston pack is the only one in the South Lakes – the other Cumbrian packs being Blencathra, Eskdale & Ennerdale, Lunesdale, Melbreak and Ullswater. Those connected with Coniston Fox Hounds meet each March at the Mortal Man Inn at Troutbeck, when a new Mayor is chosen.

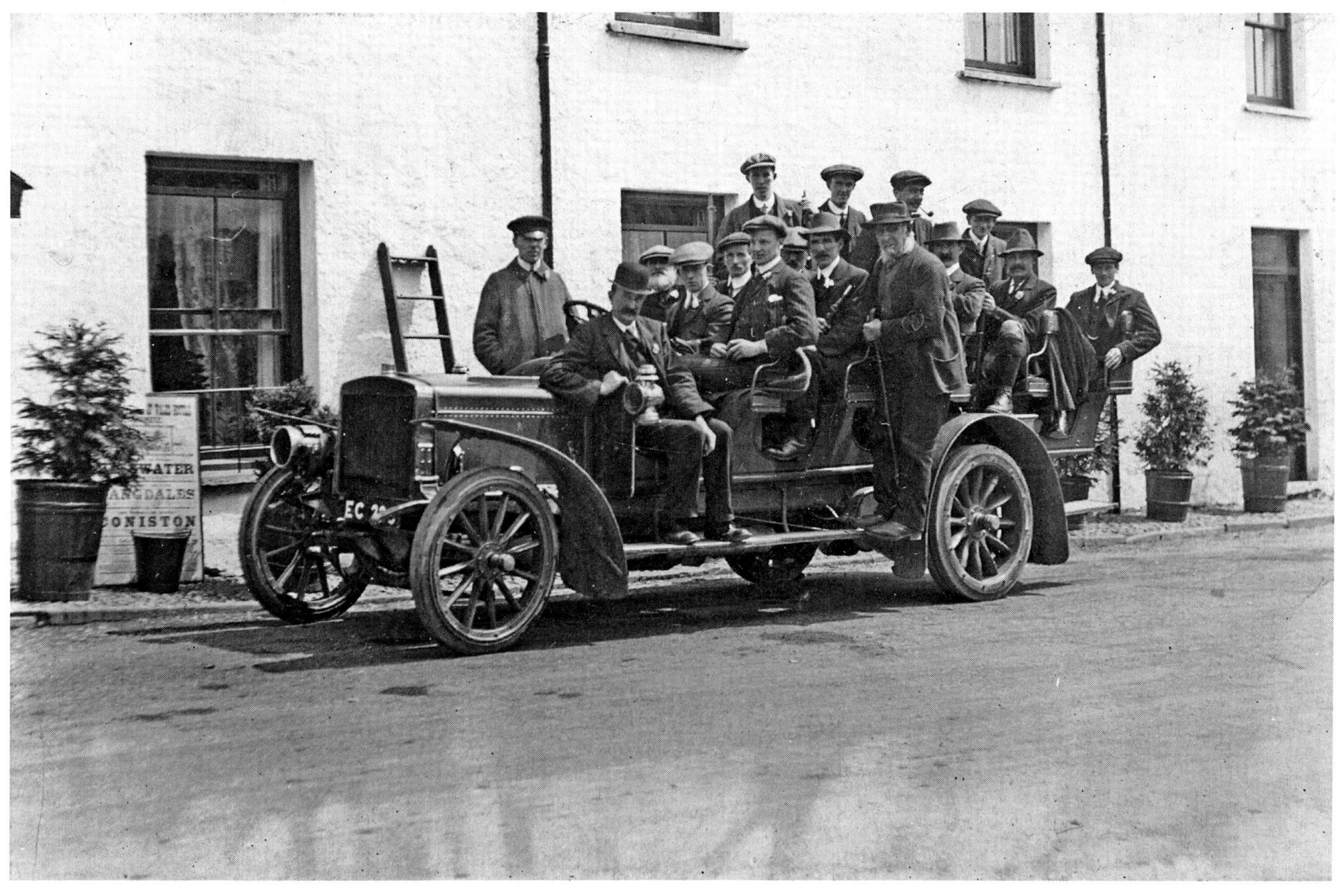

This photograph dating from 1912 or 1913, shows a well-laden tourer outside the Swan Hotel at Grasmere. Its occupants were members of the Grasmere Miniature Rifle Club, on their way to a competition at Cummersdale. The club enjoyed some success locally, but the First World War probably put an end to its activities.

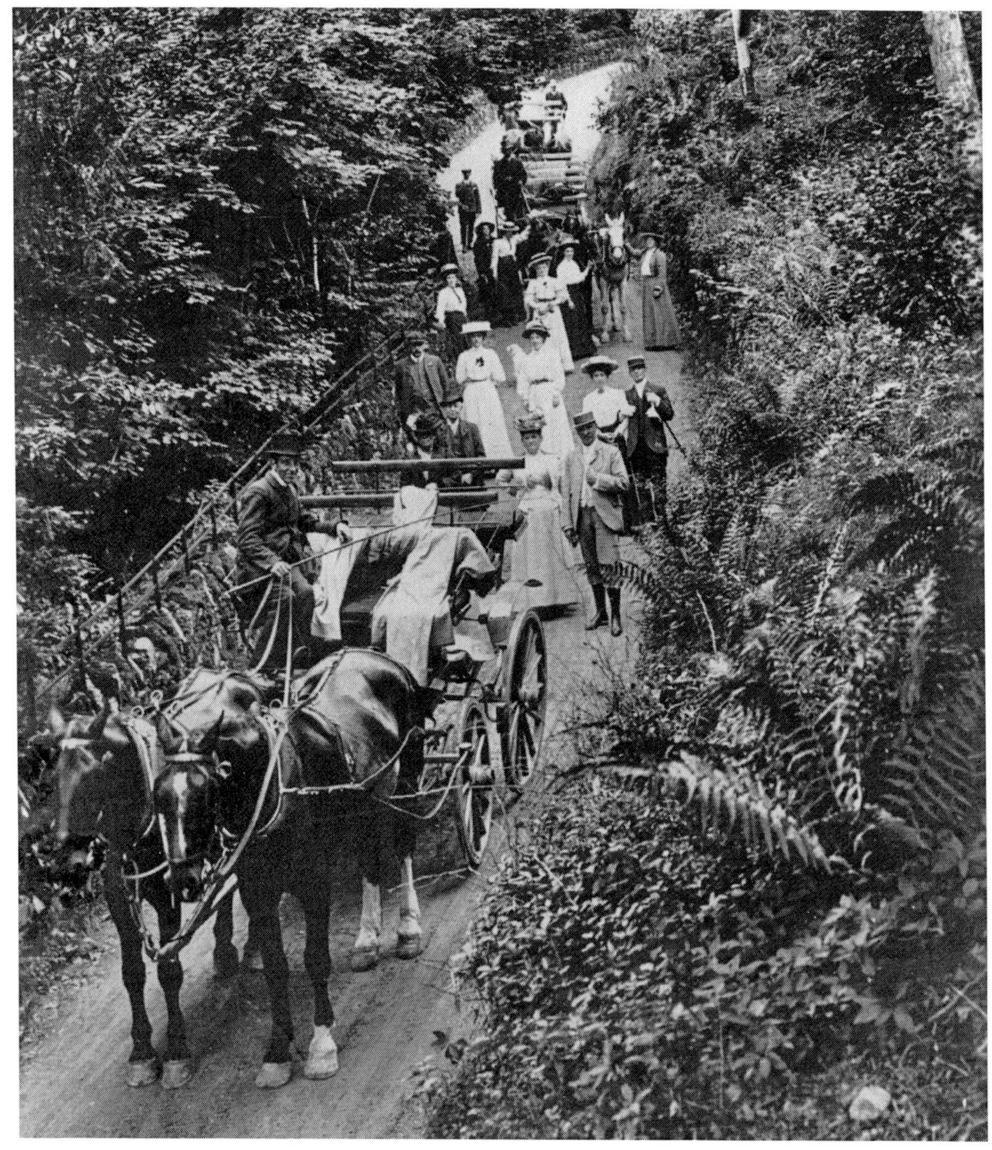

The road from Grasmere to Elterwater reaches the ridge of Hunting Stile, whence fine views of the Langdale Valley and the Langdale Pikes may be enjoyed, before dropping steeply via Red Bank. This Edwardian postcard well illustrates the perils to coach passengers on the precipitous Red Bank, who would usually have had to get out and walk to save the horses. This challenging road is well-known to the thousands of charity walkers who, each year, tramp the 40 miles or so from Keswick to Barrow.

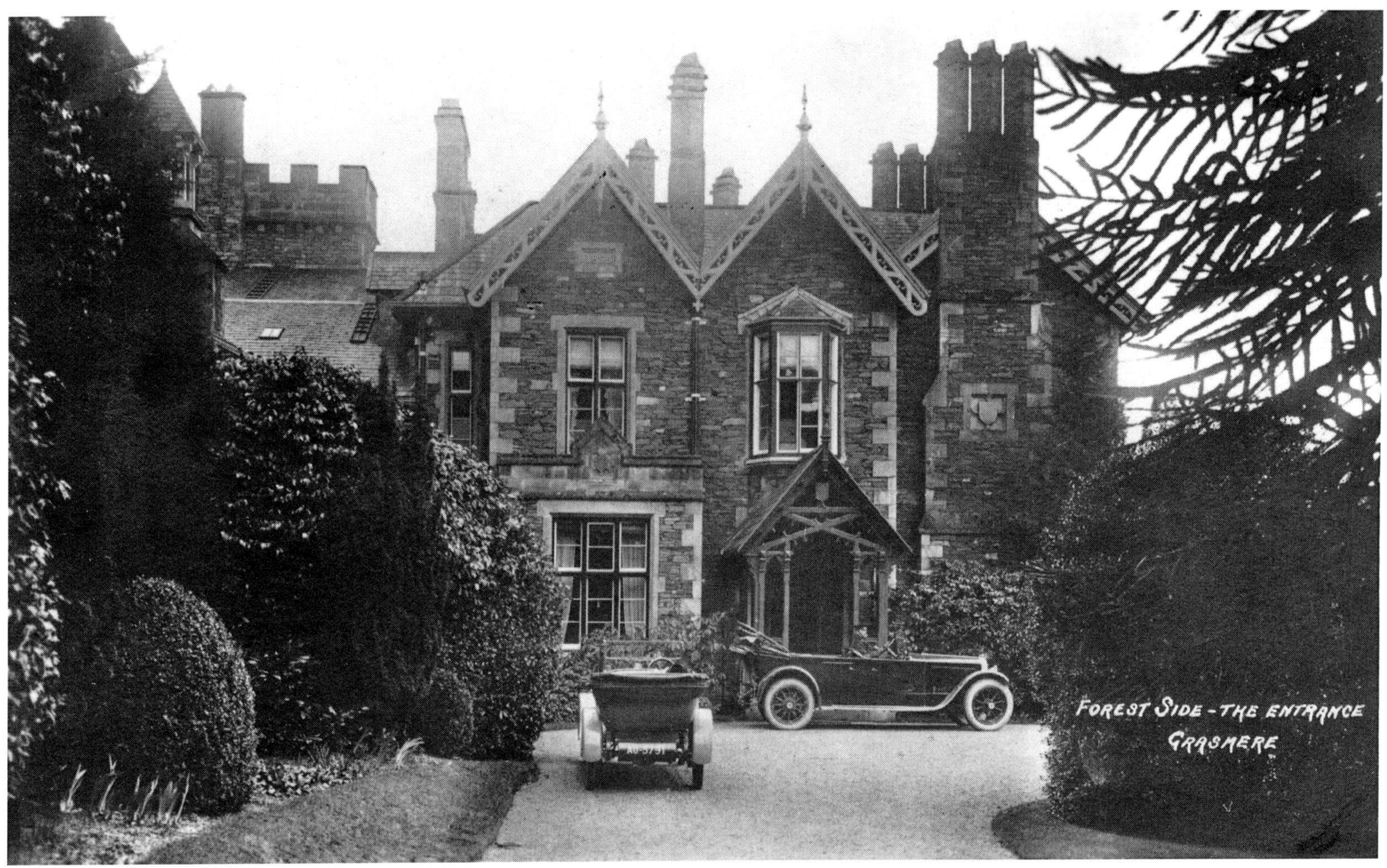

Forest Side is typical of the Lakeland mansions that were constructed after the railway came to Windermere in 1847. There was a farm here once, but the present building dates from 1853, when it was owned by a wealthy Manchester solicitor. Forest Side passed through several hands in Victorian times, including Charles Younge, a 70-year-old Sheffield businessman who purchased the property on the occasion of his marriage to a 20-year-old in 1863! The couple had a daughter the following year, but Charles died when his daughter was only three. By 1900 Forest Side was described as "commercial", and the site was acquired by the Co-operative Holidays Association in 1929. Forest Side later became a hotel, and was extensively renovated in 2014.

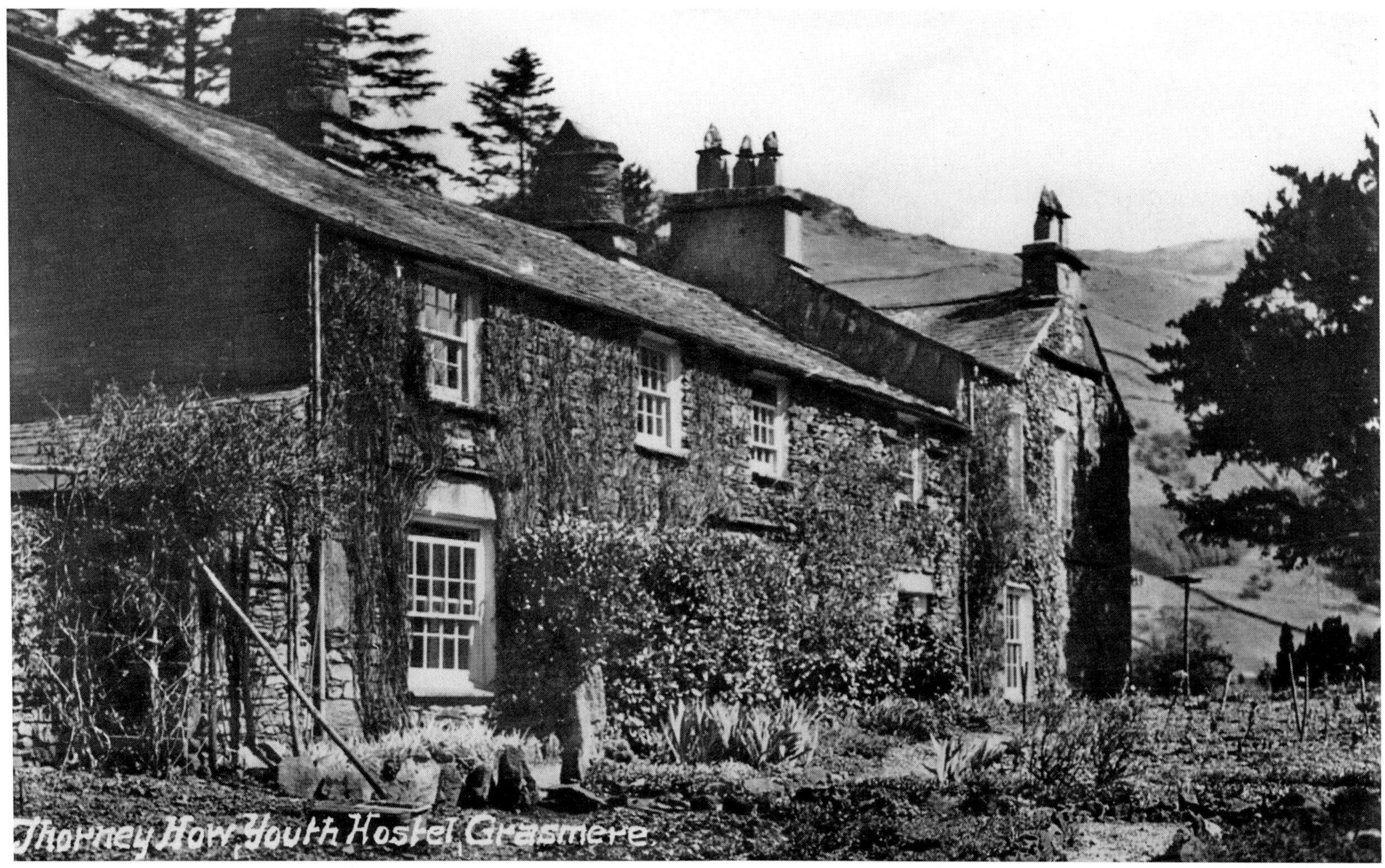

Grasmere provided, then as now, a wide range of accommodation and most visitors would have had little difficulty in finding a bed for the night. The growth in popularity of fellwalking after the First World War led to a demand for cheaper, more basic, accommodation and Thorney How was acquired by the Youth Hostel Association in 1930 and opened the following year. It has the distinction of being the first hostel fully-owned by the YHA. The building, dating from the seventeenth century, was originally a farmhouse, which was renovated and improved in Victorian times. Today, Thorney How is an independent hostel.

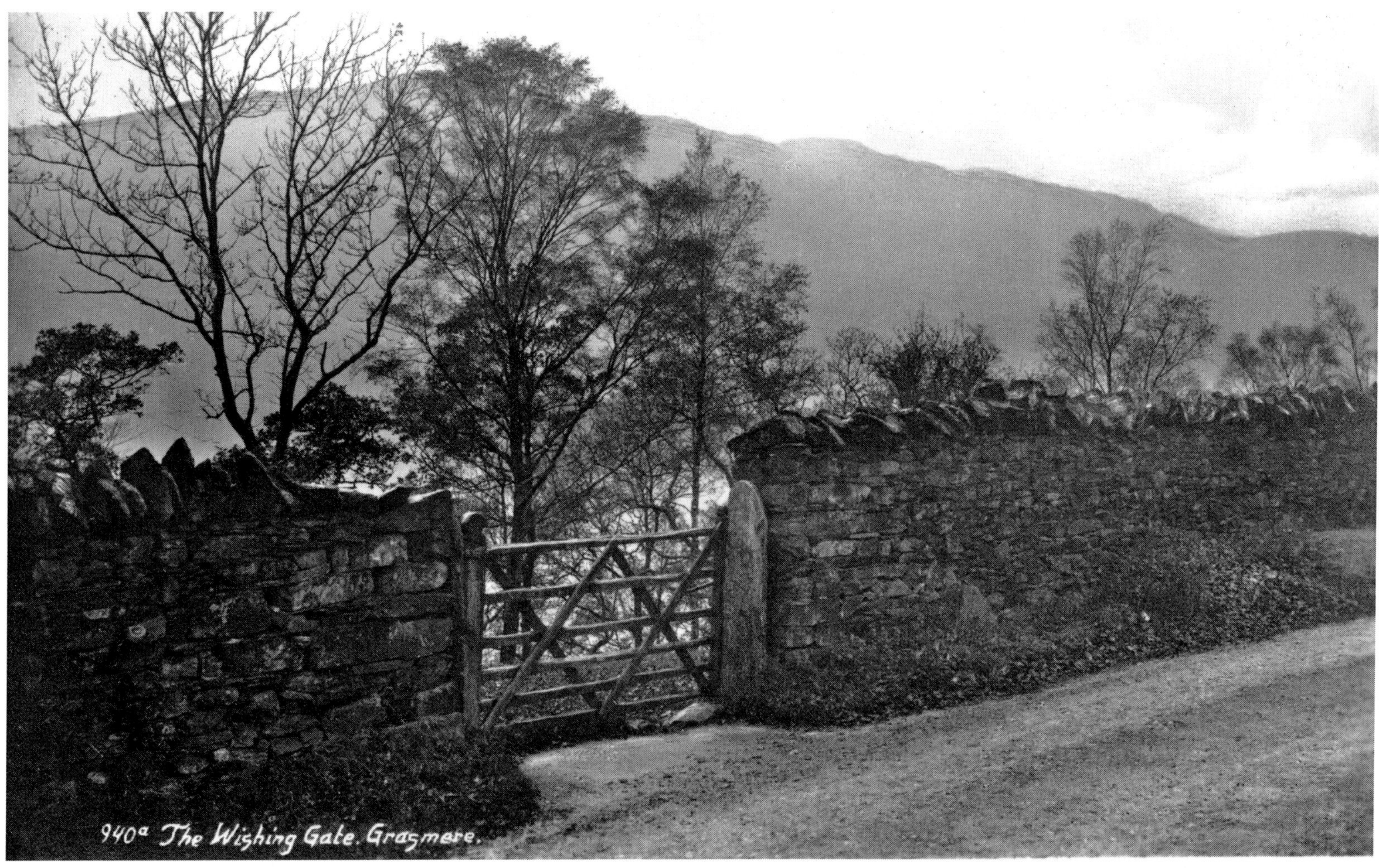

In 1828 Wordsworth wrote this introduction to a poem: "In the Vale of Grasmere, by the side of the old high-way leading to Ambleside, is a gate which, time out of mind, has been called the Wishing-gate, from a belief that wishes formed or indulged there have a favourable issue". Wordsworth had been told that the gate had been destroyed and the gap walled-up, so he lamented the gate's passing in his poem "The Wishing Gate". Sometime later, he was delighted to find that the gate was still there. In Wordsworth's family, the gate was often called "Sara's Gate", as his sister-in-law loved the view of Grasmere from the gate. The gate has been renewed since Wordsworth's day, but today's passer-by may still cast a wish!

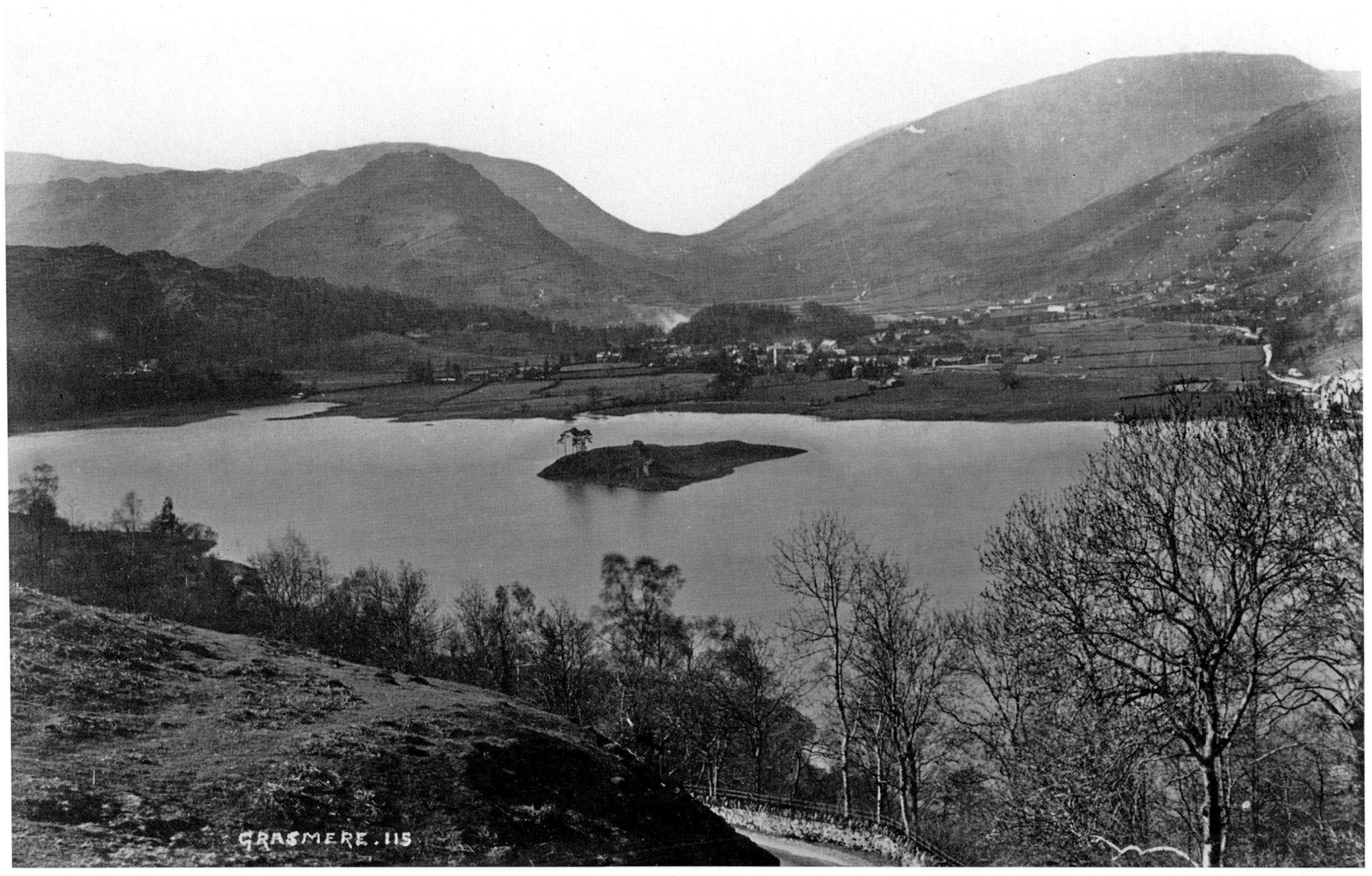

Grasmere, or "the lake flanked by grass", is one of the smaller lakes in the Lake District. It is fed and drained by the River Rothay, which flows from the village to the lake, and thence to Rydal Water and Lake Windermere. Sailing boats and rowing boats are allowed to use the lake, but not power boats. There is a small island, which is known as The Island! Imaginative folk hereabouts! There are a number of gentle walks around and above the lake, much enjoyed by many a visitor.

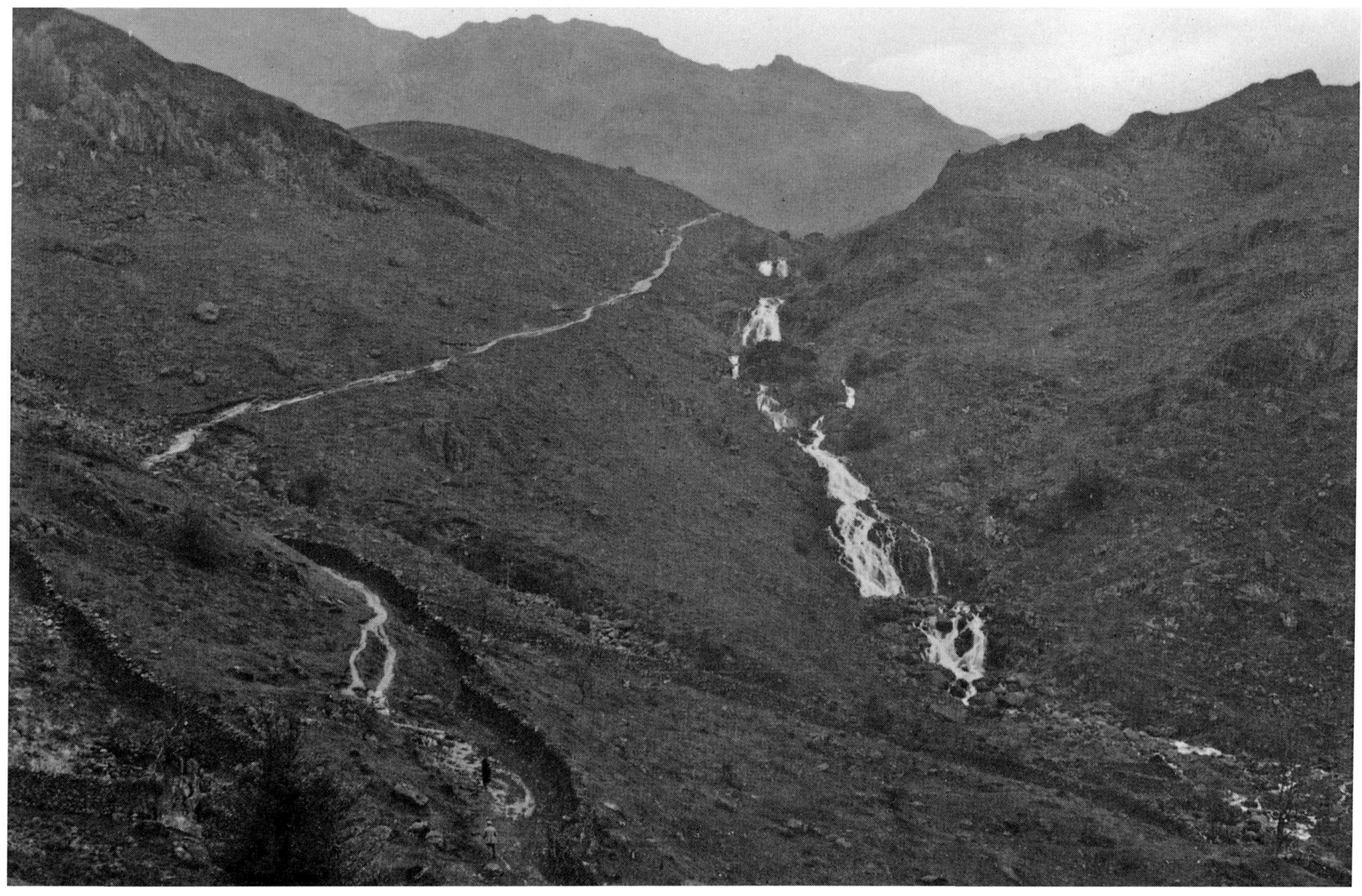

From Grasmere, the track to Easedale Tarn rises gradually to Sour Milk Ghyll and its waterfall. The falls owe their curious name to the colour of the turbulent water, which, to some, resembles white churning milk. Dorothy Wordsworth likened the falls to "a broad stream of white snow". The waterfall is the outflow from Easedale Tarn.

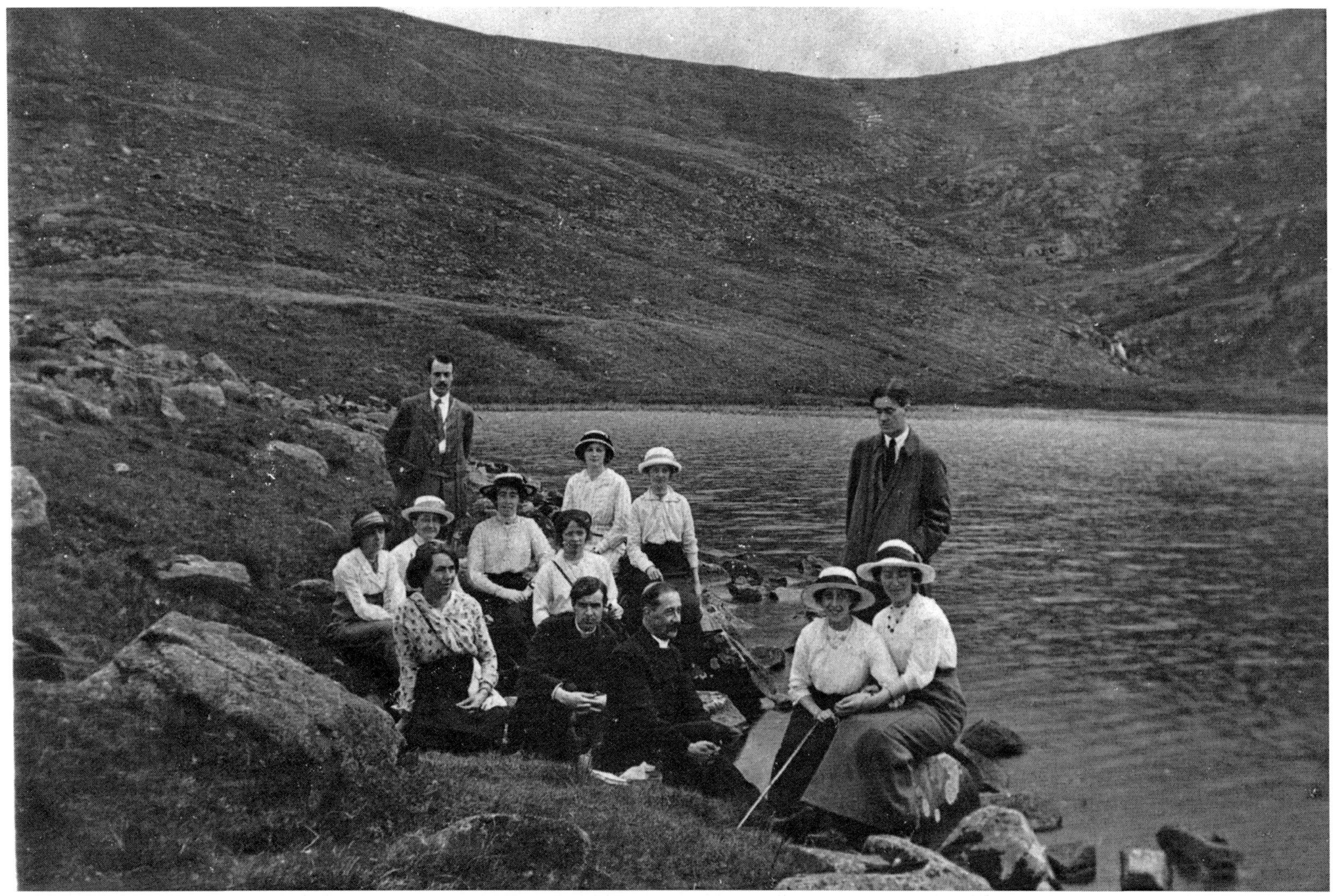

In Victorian and Edwardian times those tourists seeking a modest walk on the lower-lying fells near Grasmere village would often make their way to Easedale Tarn where, as this Edwardian photo shows, they could relax by the water or perhaps paint or sketch.

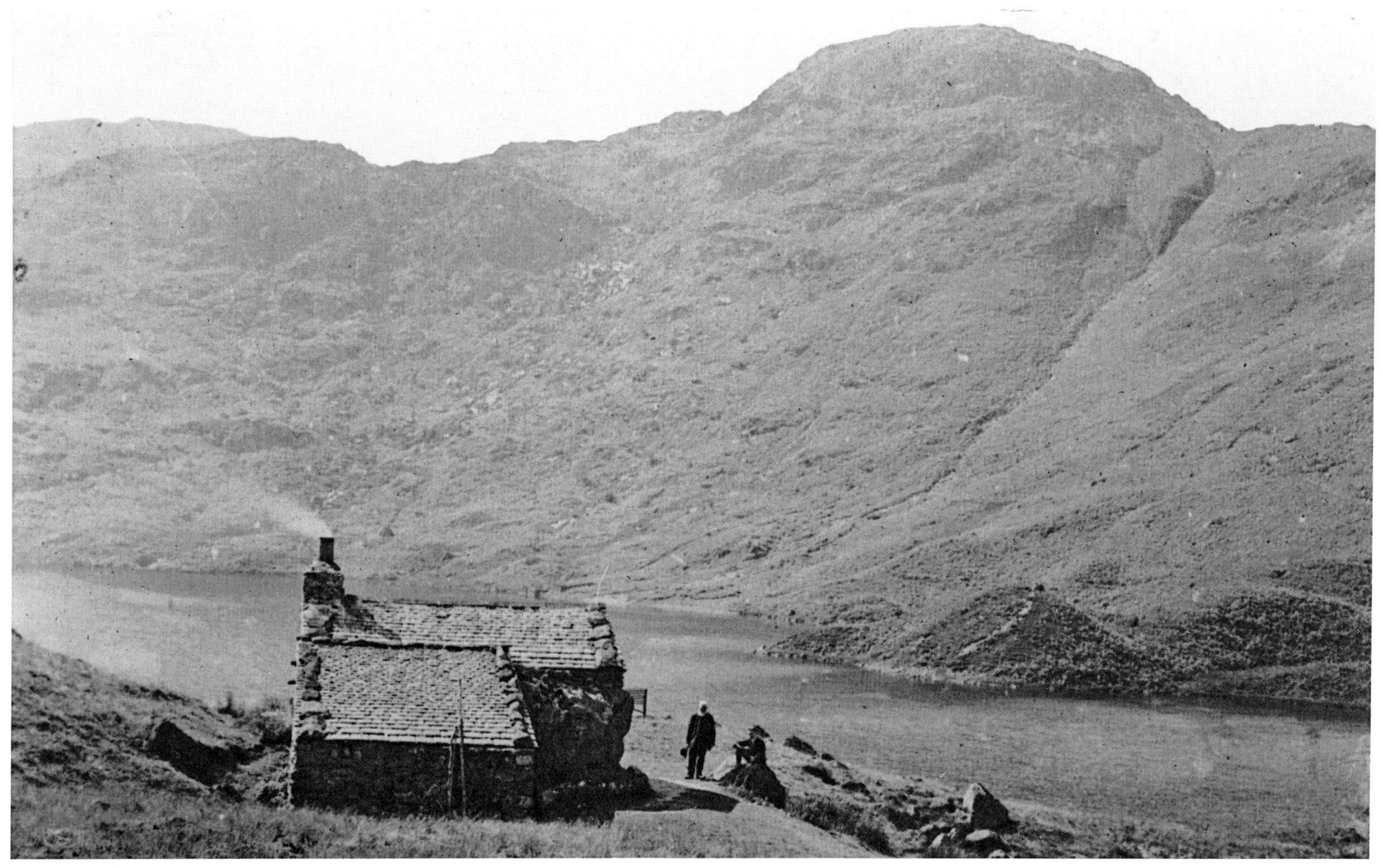

Towards the end of the nineteenth century, a certain Richard Hayton constructed a refreshment hut on higher ground near the tarn. As the photo suggests, the hut was a rough-and-ready build, and one of the walls incorporated a huge boulder which just happened to be there! The hut was used until the 1930s, but after the Second World War it fell into disrepair and was finally demolished in the 1960s. The most famous occupant of the refreshment hut was an elderly Grasmere resident, William Wilson. He provided basic refreshments, such as sandwiches, and bacon and eggs, for the visitors, and he also hired out a small boat to any adventurous tourist who fancied a row on the tarn!

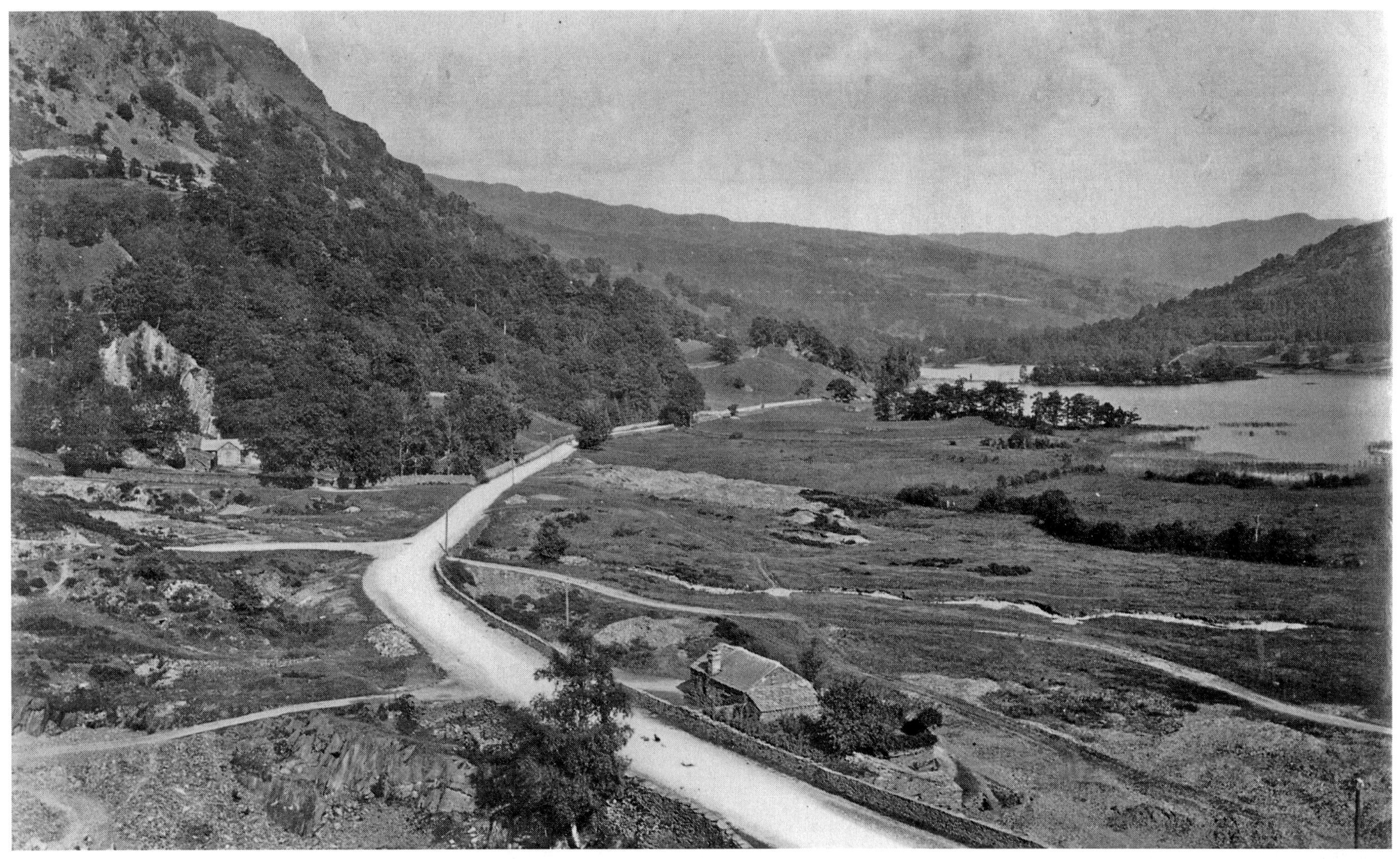

This Edwardian photo shows the Grasmere-Rydal road at White Moss Common, which was improved when the aqueduct was being constructed from Thirlmere to bring water to a thirsty Manchester. The building in the foreground is the Cascade Hotel, a refreshment hut described on the next page. There was also a "Mission on the Common", which was constructed for the navvies in 1889. Services were held every Thursday by the Reverend Stock, the vicar of Ambleside. Rydal Water, one of the smallest lakes, is on the right. Originally known as Routhmere (after the Rothay), Rydal Water is part–owned by Rydal Hall and the Lowther Estate, which leases its half to the National Trust. Boating is not allowed on the lake, unless you are a resident of Rydal Hall! Rydal Cave, a former quarry, may be found on the fell above the lake.

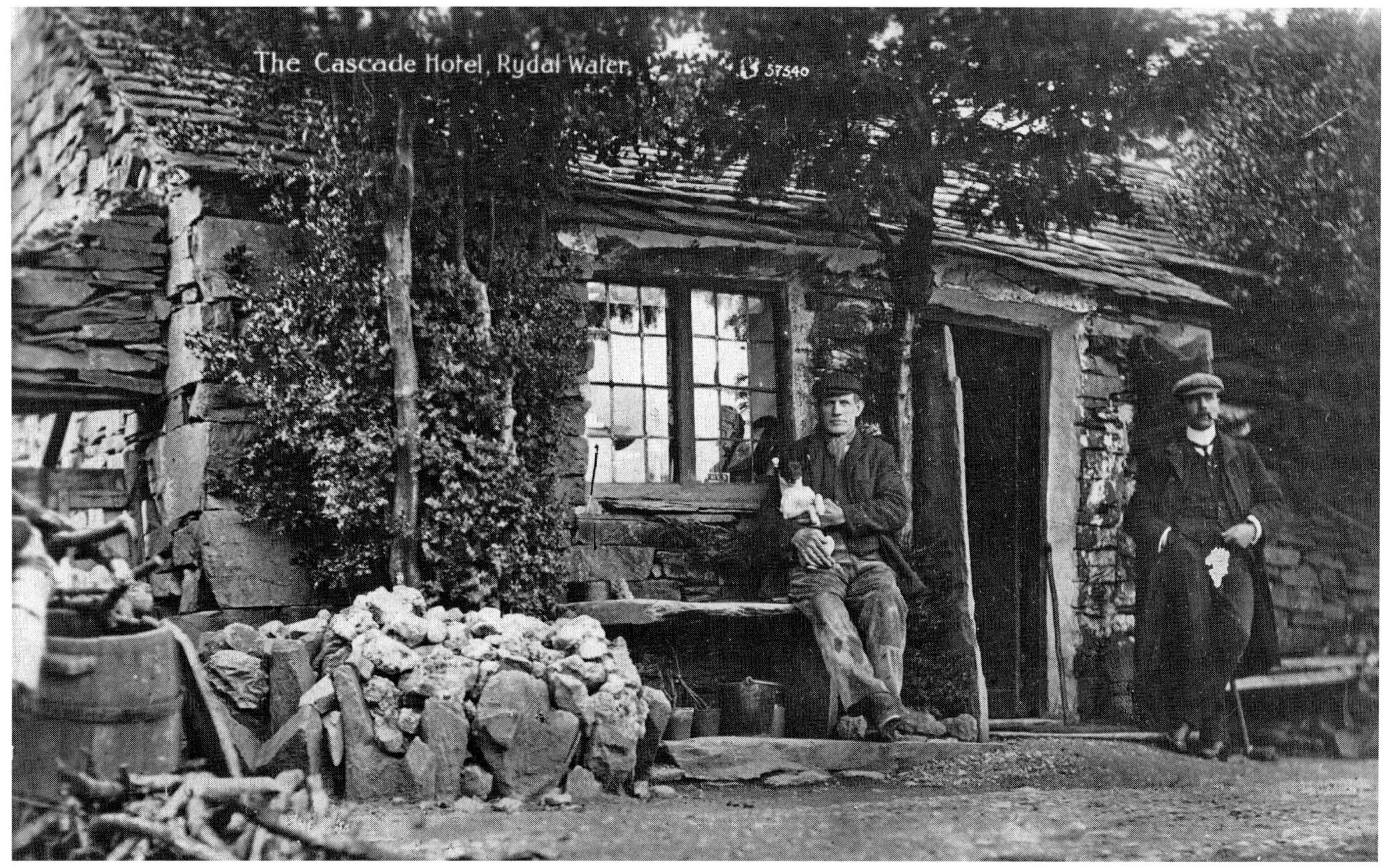

This rare early Valentine's Series postcard shows "The Cascade Hotel", a grandly-named refreshment hut which was established on the newly-constructed A591. The hut was named after the water cascade in the nearby quarry, and it was run by William Huddleston, or "Old Bill" as he was often known. He served mainly mineral water and sweets to visitors, and also pears, when in season, from a tree in the garden. The photo, which dates from around 1905, shows two men and a dog, hardly the clientele to rival that of the nearby Prince of Wales Hotel! All traces of the hut have long since disappeared.

Lines Written on
"Wordsworth's Seat," Rydal,

WHILST ON A WALKING TOUR TO GRASMERE,
MAY, 1905.

Not to seek for inspiration,
   Do I thus these steps ascend;
But to stay the perspiration,
   Which in copious drops descend.

Tired, footsore, weak and weary,
   Here I've come at last to rest;
Though alone I am not dreary,
   For the scene is at its best.

Here I sit and think of Wordsworth,
   Poet of the Lake and Fell;
For each brook, and wood, and moorland,
   Had for him a magic spell.

Rydal's waters lave before me,
   Knabb Scarr's crags they frown behind;
Loughrigg's summit—Rothay's murmur,
   Bring the poet to my mind.

Place of ever-changing beauty,
   In all seasons of the year;
Ever vernal, ever lovely,
   And to me for ever dear.

13, Calton Terrace,   WILLIAM TROUGHTON.
Morecambe.

NOTE.—A copy of the above has been most graciously
accepted by Mrs. Wordsworth, of Rydal Mount.

Wordsworth lived at Rydal Mount from 1813 until his death in 1850. He is reputed to have sat on this large rock overlooking Rydal Water, and years later a Morecambe man, William Troughton, dedicated this poem to his hero. The rock is so close to the busy A591 that anyone sitting on it nowadays would be able to contemplate only the heavy volume of traffic during the tourist season!

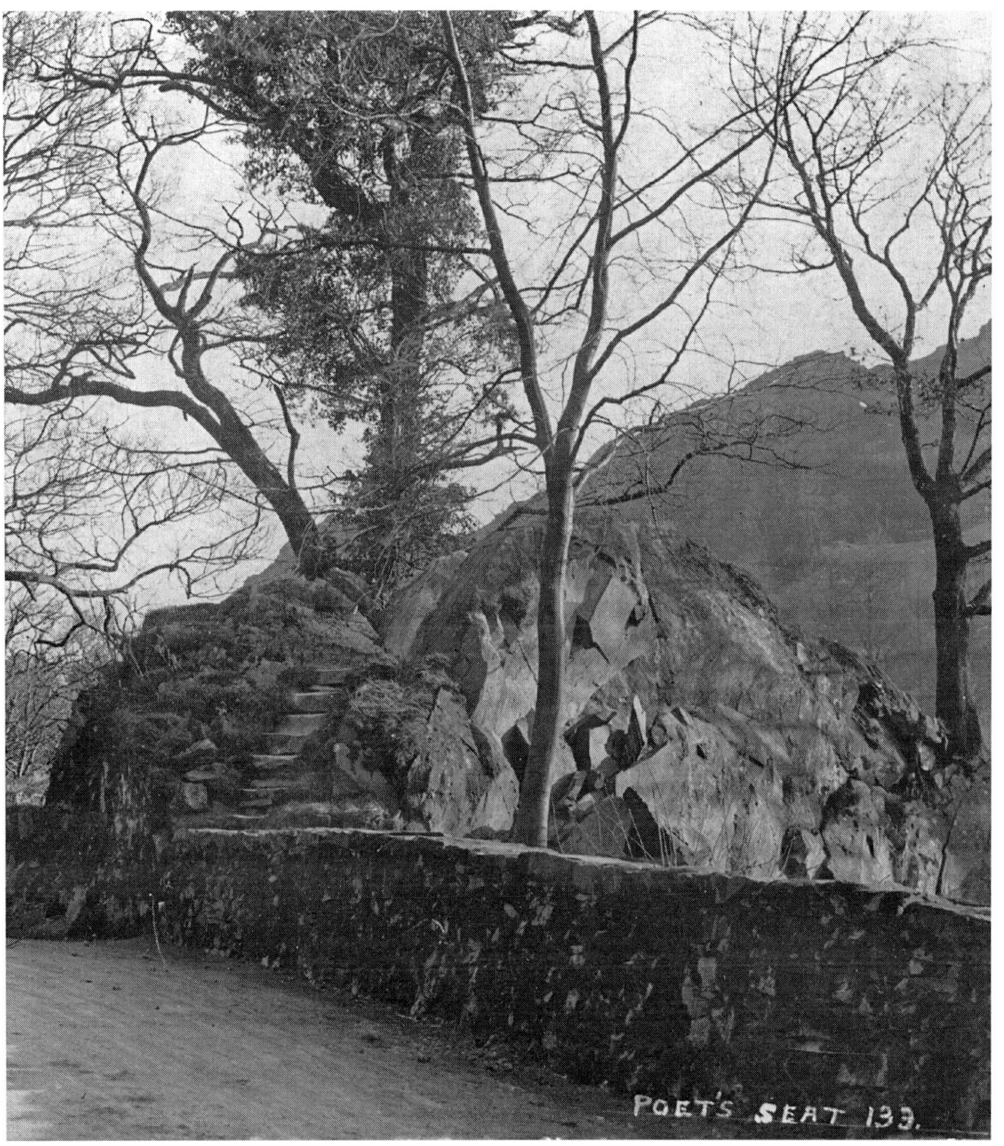

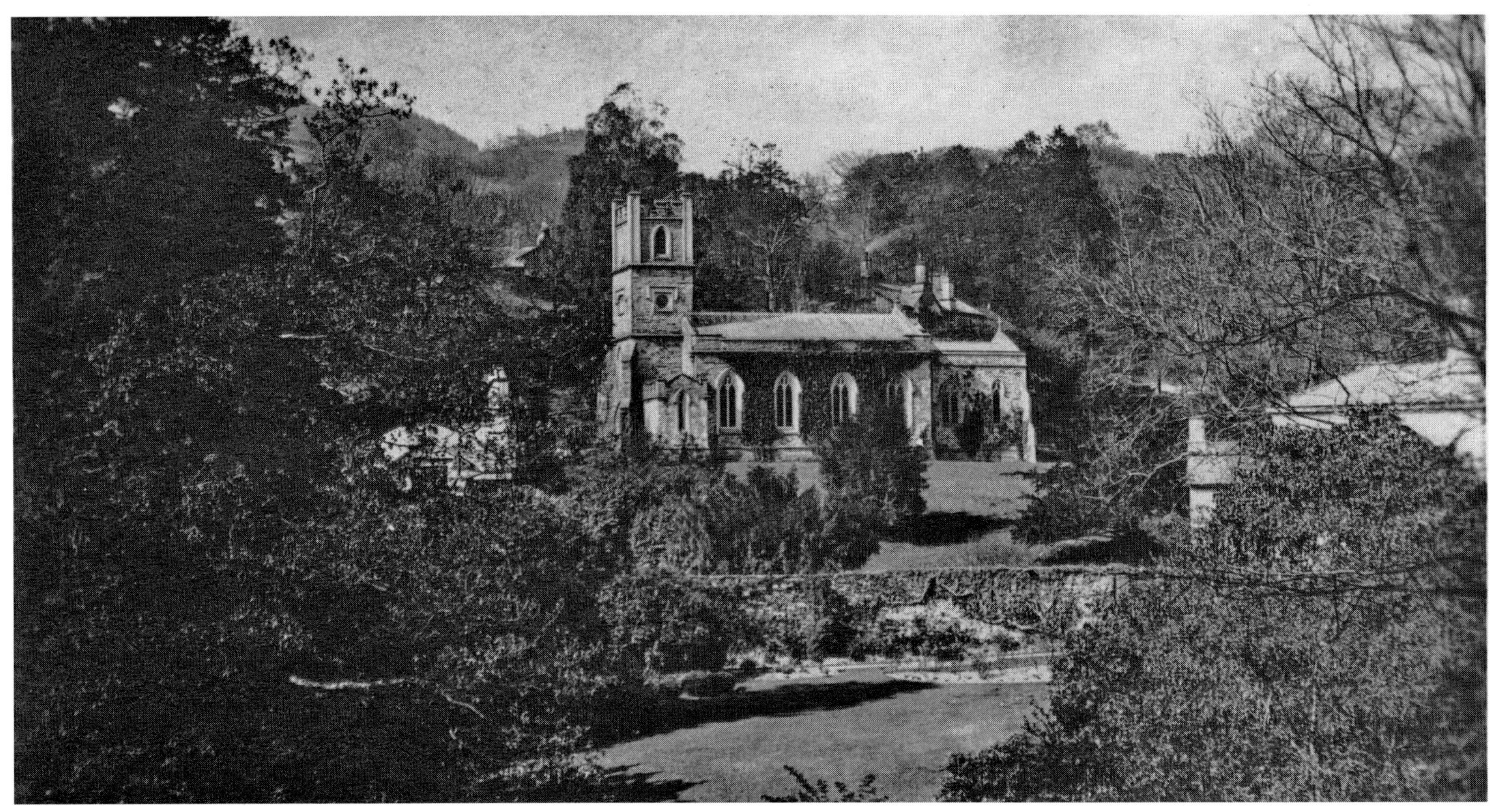

In the eighteenth century, Grasmere and Rydal were remote communities, but by the early 1800s the growing local population needed new churches. In 1823, Lady Fleming of Rydal Hall laid the foundation stone for the Chapel of St Mary at Rydal, and the inaugural service took place on Christmas Day, 1824. William Wordsworth, who leased nearby Rydal Mount from Lady Fleming, was a keen supporter of the new church, and in 1833 he served as Chapelwarden. Restoration and improvements were made to the church in 1881 and more recently in 1992. Rydal Church comprises chancel and nave, a vestry, a northern porch leading to a gallery and the tower, with its clock and single bell. The interior of the church is quite plain, but the stained-glass windows are worthy of examination. The east window commemorates members of the Fleming family, while the other three remember Dr Arnold of Rugby and his wife (with a separate memorial to their ten children), Dora Wordsworth (the poet's sister), and Wilson Fox, a local physician. The Arnold pew faces the lectern, whilst that used by the Wordsworths faces the pulpit. William last attended church on Sunday 10th March, 1850, dying just over two weeks later, shortly after his eightieth birthday. He and his family are buried at Grasmere, as Rydal Church was built on a rocky outcrop, making burials impractical.

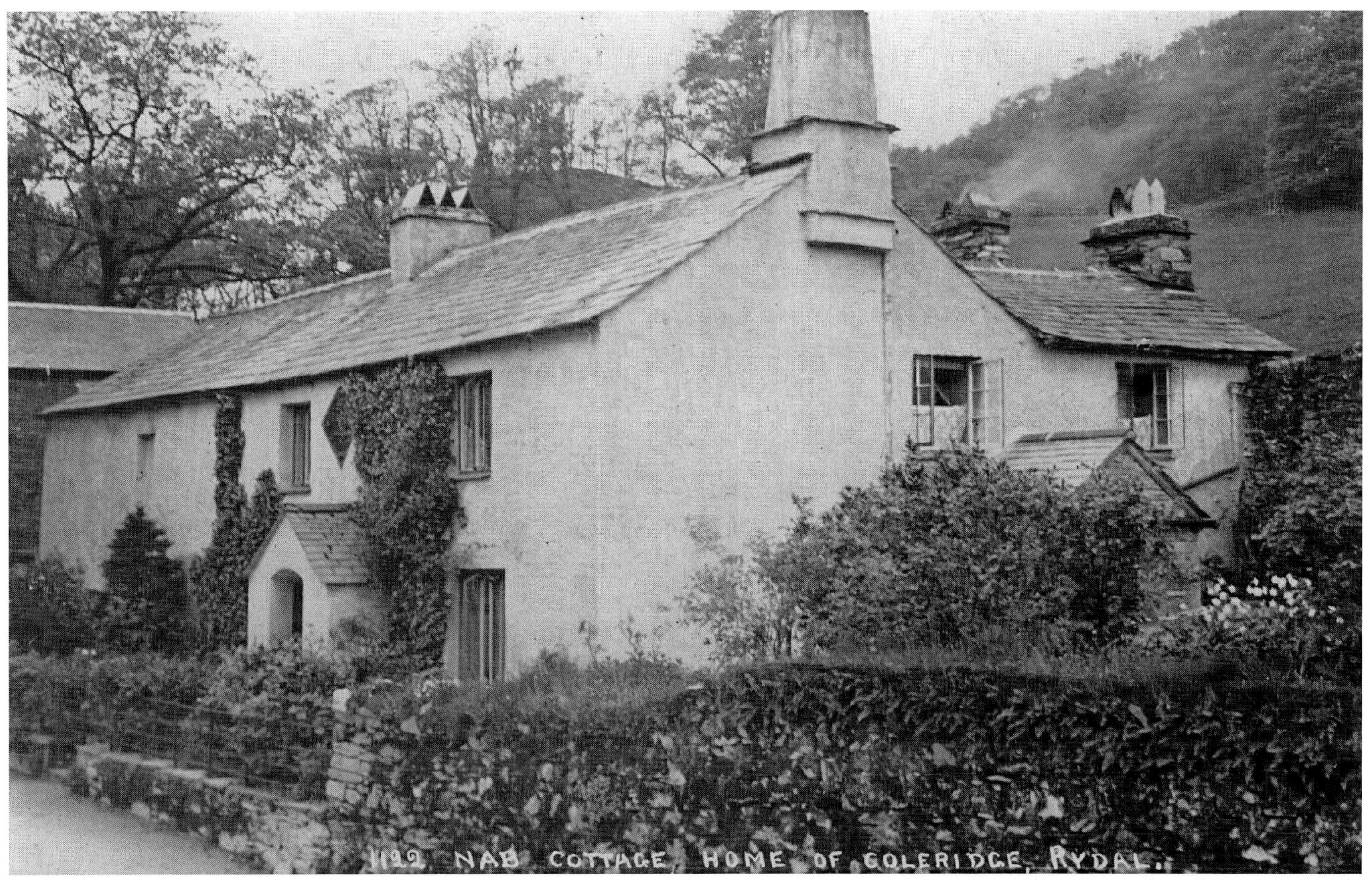

This Lakeland farmhouse dates from 1565 or 1566, but it was extended by John Parke in 1702 and continued to be a working farm until the 1940s. In 1817 Thomas de Quincy, author of Confessions of an English Opium Eater and a friend of Wordsworth, moved in with his new wife. They remained there until 1833, when the writer's opium addiction and debt forced the de Quincys to move to Edinburgh, whereupon the farm was leased to David Hartley Coleridge, son of the famous poet. More recently, the fields were sold, and Nab Cottage became a bed & breakfast establishment.

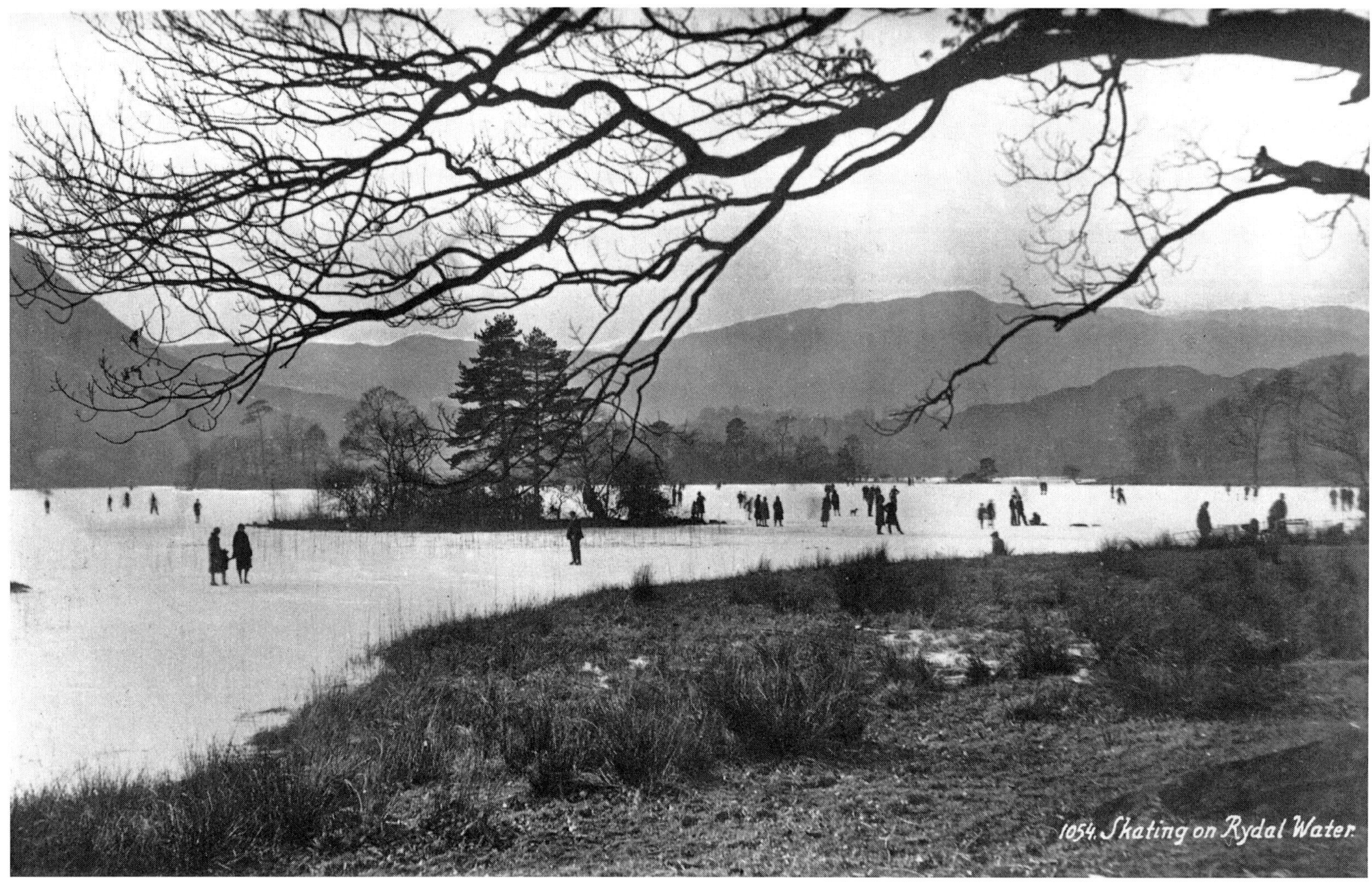

In the England of the twenty-first century, winters are generally mild, and even the smaller lakes do not freeze over in the colder months, but this was not so a hundred years ago, as this Edwardian postcard of Rydal Water clearly shows. In those days, every lake and tarn would freeze over and the locals could look forward to skating on the ice. On the larger lakes, such as nearby Windermere, it would not have been unusual to see stagecoaches and motor cars driving on the thick ice.

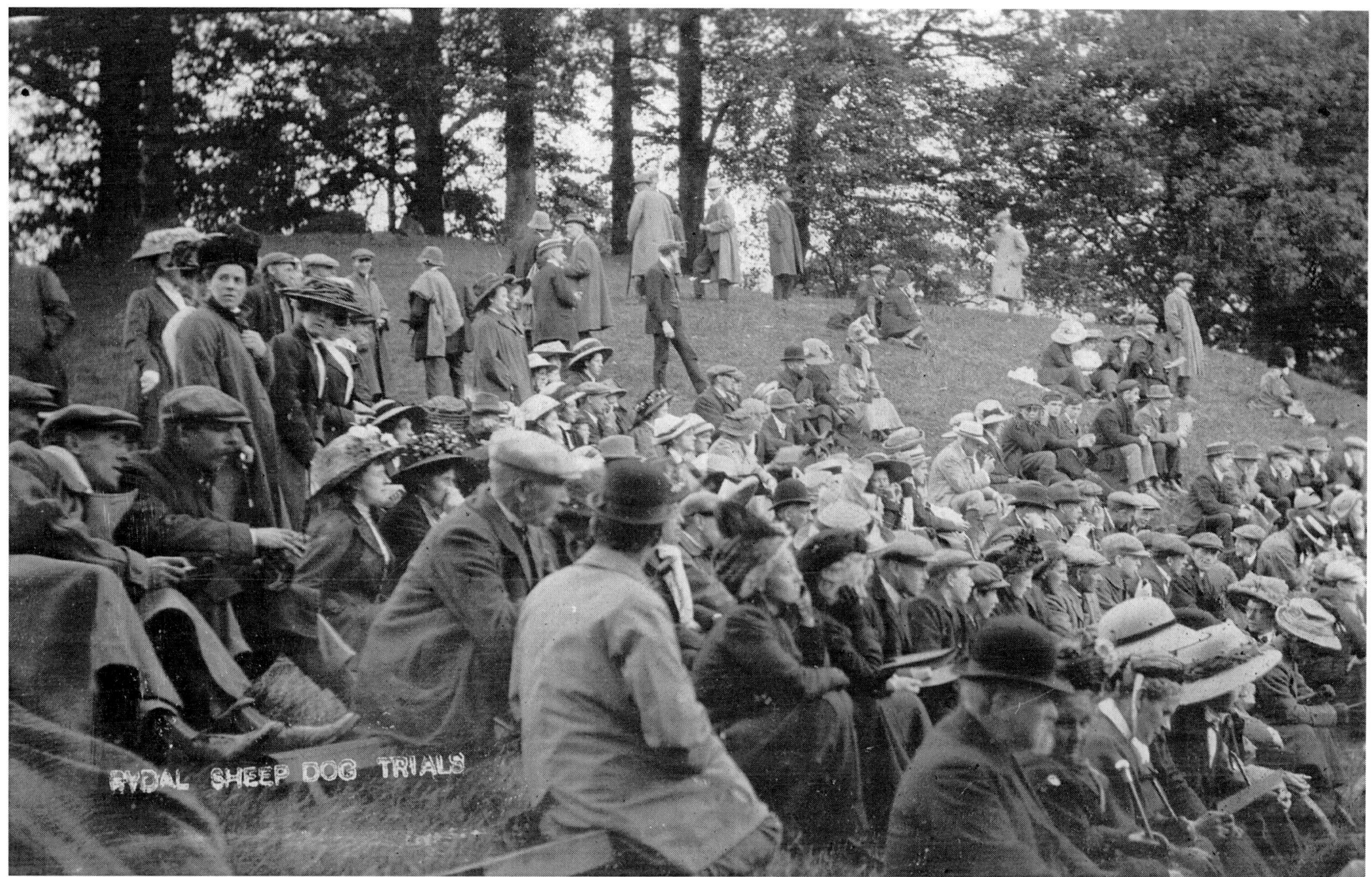

The Vale of Rydal Sheepdog Trials were first held at Rydal Park on 13th June, 1901, having been organised by a committee of volunteers under the patronage of Stanley le Fleming, whose family has continued to support the event. The postcard shows spectators watching the trials sometime before the First World War. Hound shows and other events have been added to the programme over the years, and in 1931 the Trials became the first Lakeland event to be broadcast worldwide on the wireless.

Accommodation at Rydal was always more difficult to find than at Grasmere, but for many years the Glen Rothay Hotel has been catering for tourists. Parts of the building date back to the 1700s, when it was called "David's Inn". It became a private residence called "Ivy Cottage", before being extended in Victorian times. In the 1930s the proprietor boasted that the hotel was situated in "beautiful wooded grounds overlooking Rydal Water and adjoining the grounds of the late poet Wordsworth." The sender of this postcard in the 1950s praised the hotel's "excellent food and service."

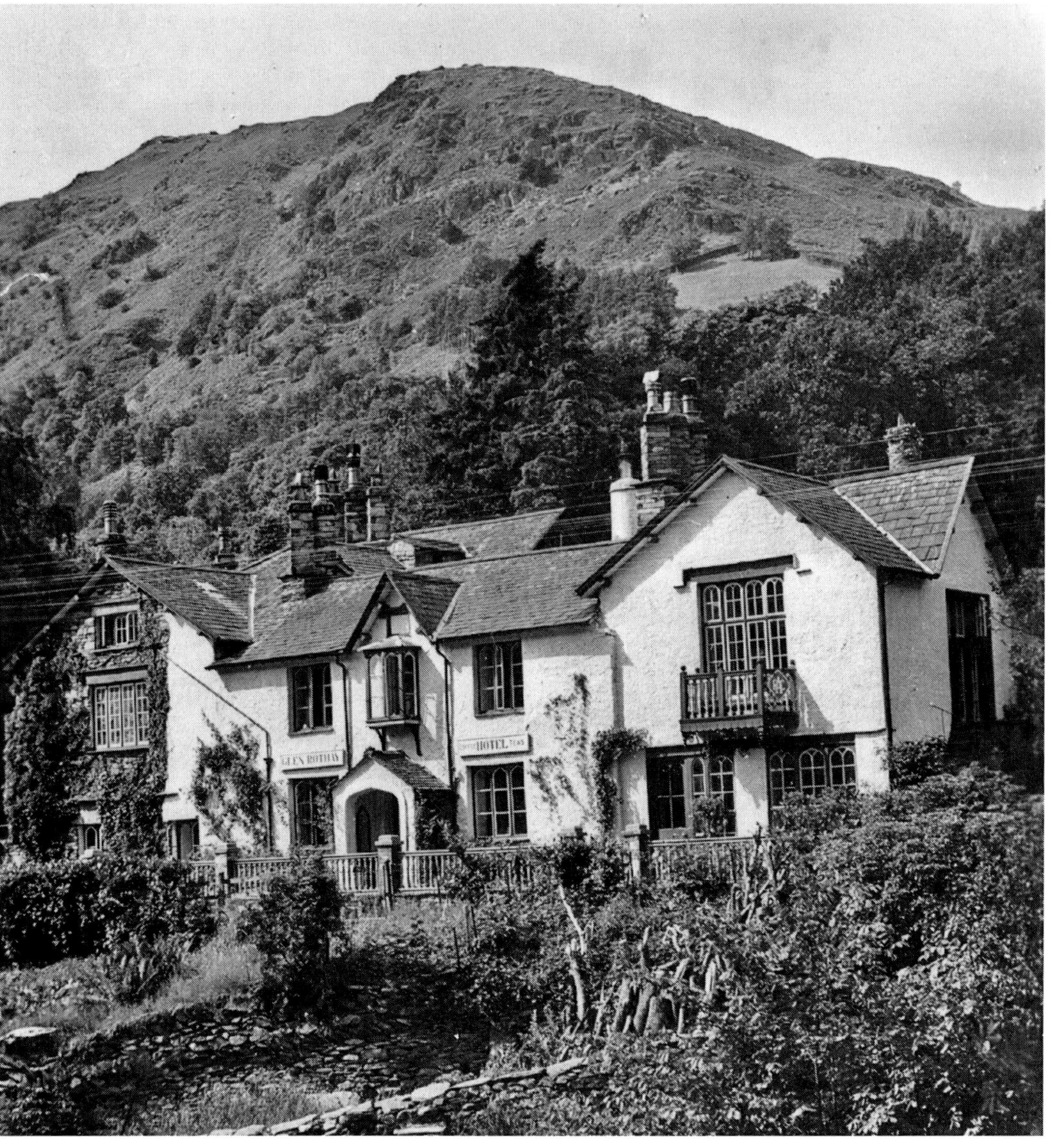

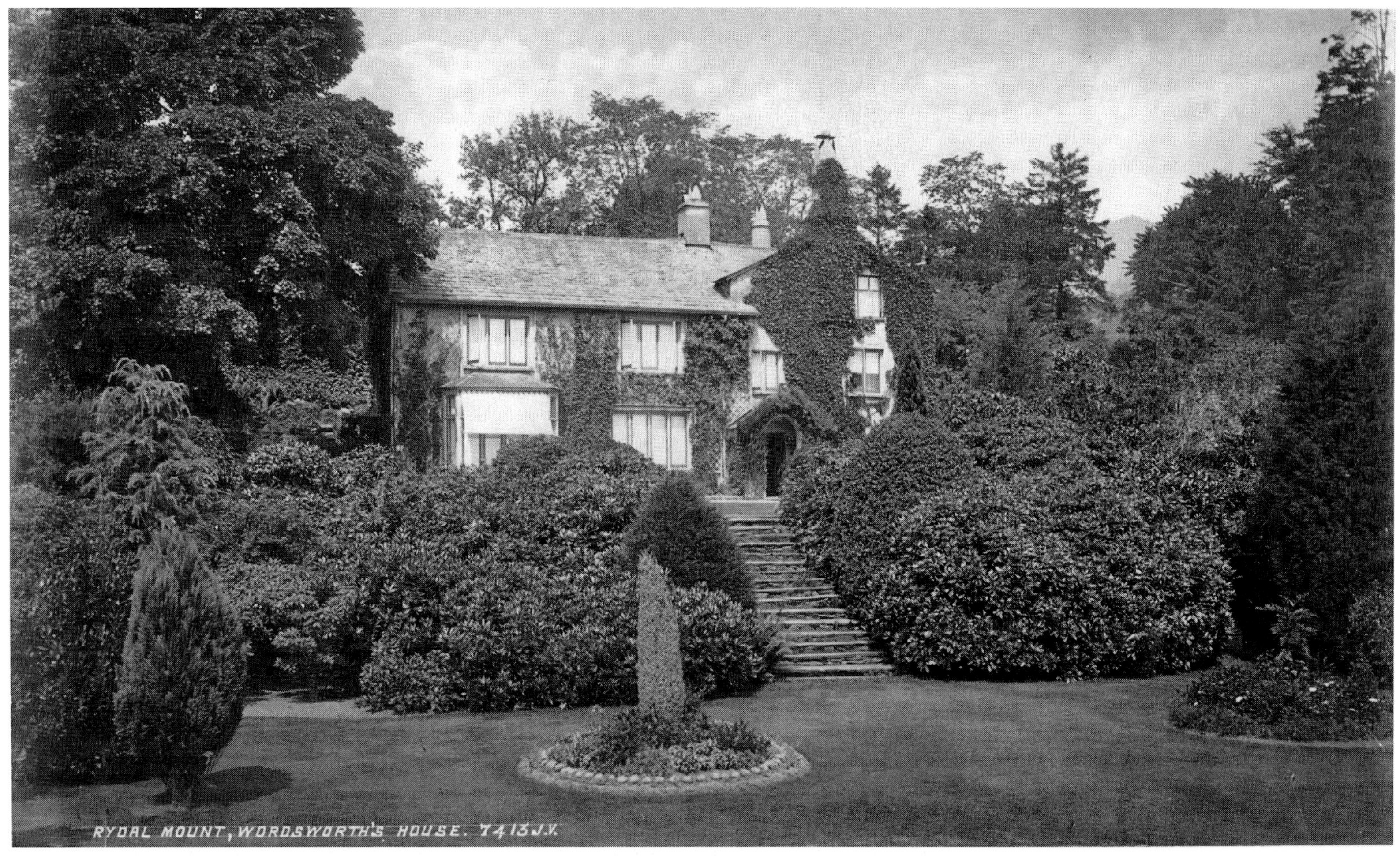

Rydal Mount was the Wordsworth's family home from 1813 until 1859, the year in which Mary Wordsworth died. Wordsworth had rented the property from Lady le Fleming of Rydal Hall, paying a year's rent of just £35 in 1822! An original Tudor cottage was extended in 1750, and Wordsworth designed the gardens and built a simple "writing hut" in which to work. He loved the views of Grasmere and Windermere enjoyed from the upper gardens, and was often visited by his friend, the poet Samuel Taylor Coleridge, who would walk to Rydal Mount from his home in Keswick. In 1969, Wordsworth's great-great-granddaughter, Mary Henderson, purchased Rydal Mount and it remains to this day in the hands of the Wordsworth family. It was opened to the public in 1970.

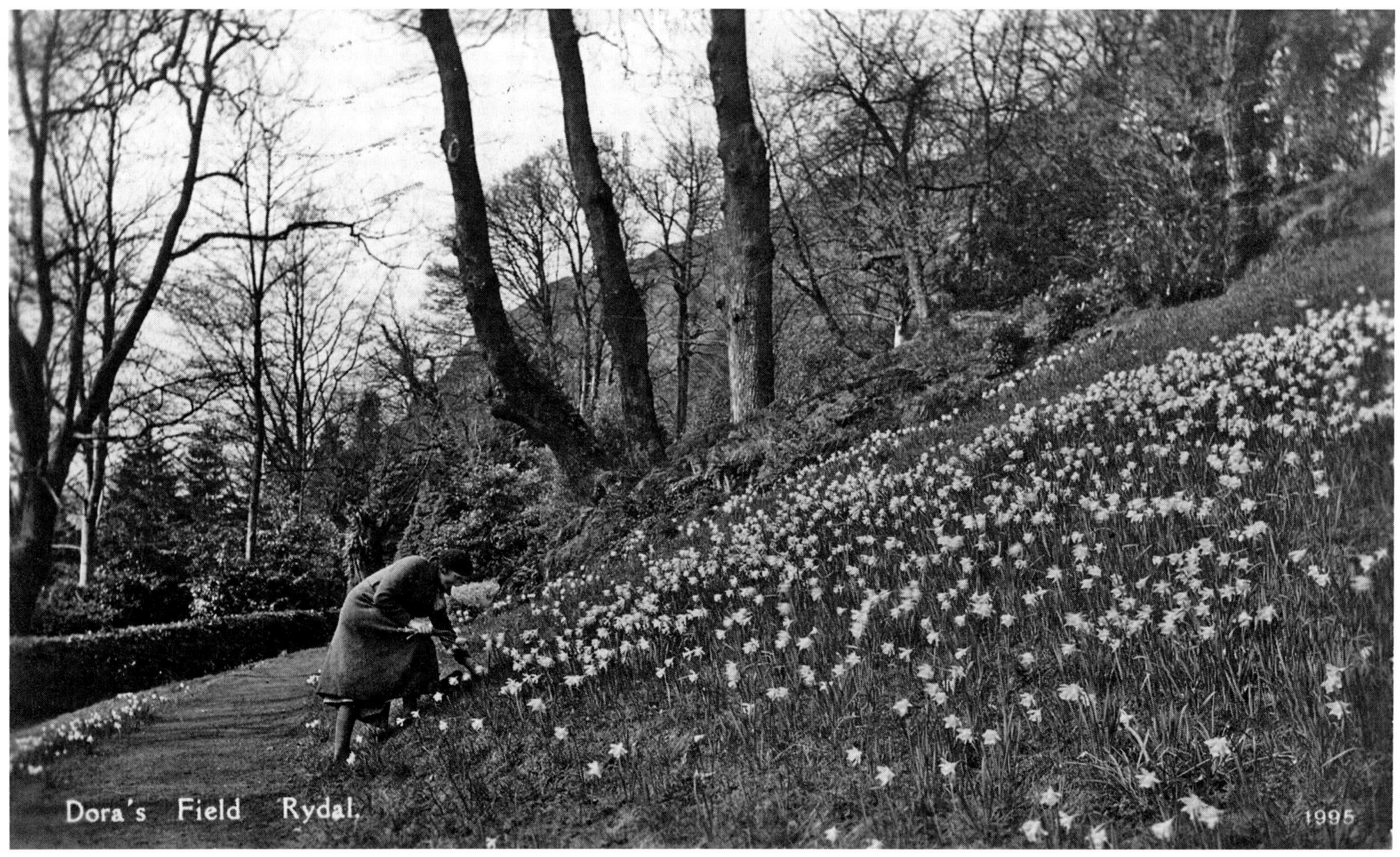

Relations between Wordsworth and his landlady were not always cordial – he often complained about damp in the property – and in 1825 she threatened to rent Rydal Mount to a relative. The riposte was swift: in 1826 Wordsworth purchased the Rash Field next to the church, intending to build a house on it and in doing, blocking the view from Rydal Mount. Lady le Fleming thereupon withdrew her threat and the house was never built. In 1847, just three years before the poet's death, Dora, his only surviving daughter, died of tuberculosis and he renamed the field "Dora's Field", planting hundreds of daffodils in her memory. In 1935 Dora's Field was sold to the National Trust, and so the public may now enjoy the splendid displays of daffodils and bluebells when in season.